THE
REAL
DEAL

THE
REAL
DEAL

MY DECADE FIGHTING BATTLES AND
WINNING WARS WITH TRUMP

GEORGE A. SORIAL

AND DAMIAN BATES

BROADSIDE BOOKS
An Imprint of HarperCollins*Publishers*

HarperCollins books may be purchased for educational, business, or sales promotional use. For information, please email the Special Markets Department at SPsales@harpercollins.com.

Broadside Books™ and the Broadside logo are trademarks of HarperCollins Publishers.

FIRST EDITION

Library of Congress Cataloging-in-Publication Data has been applied for.

ISBN 978-0-06-288766-5

19 20 21 22 23   LSC   10 9 8 7 6 5 4 3 2 1

To our families and friends with love

Have I not commanded you? Be strong and of good courage; do not be afraid, nor be dismayed, for the Lord your God is with you wherever you go.

—*Joshua 1:9*

Contents

CHAPTER 1

The Golden Years

The gray clouds on the New York City horizon were mirrored by the metaphorical ones hovering over the economy as the price of a barrel of oil floated around the $50 mark. The talk was of an impending recession.

At Trump Tower, however, over on Fifth and Fifty-Seventh, the outlook on this overcast day in 2006 was very different. The future looked bright. Outside the massive atrium of this golden temple of commerce, many remembered a huge banner that previously flew proud, bearing the unforgettable slogan "You're Fired!" Underneath, in more muted tones, it thanked the people of New York for helping to make the biggest new TV show of the year possible. It wasn't that long ago that a staggering twenty-eight million people watched Thursday night's *The Apprentice* as it reached its climax in its debut season.

Splashed across that brash, bright banner was one man walking intently toward the camera. He was the star of the show and the one figure on which all the fuss was focused. He was gaining reams of column inches in magazines and newspapers, more coverage than he'd ever seen before. They all wanted to interview The Donald. The show was attracting younger viewers with college educations who earned good money. It was proving a TV triumph and bringing new attention to what would become one of the biggest and most controversial brands—not to mention names—on the planet.

The Trump Organization was riding high, enjoying the plaudits, attention, and free publicity that came with the boss being plastered all over the nation's screens week in, week out, as season followed successful season of the hit show. The accelerating success was a result of the incredible publicity that came with that groundbreaking TV show and its brash, fearsome, direct leader. Not everyone wanted to do business with Donald J. Trump, of course, but the organization was being swamped with offers, ideas, and requests from all over the globe. *The Apprentice* was arguably the best thing to ever happen to The Trump Organization, and it made the business the global brand it is today.

I remember those times, and that specific day so clearly, because I stepped into that maelstrom of ideas and talent, and it changed my life.

In the beginning, I felt more than a little out of place. I

was a quiet guy who had been taught by monks at a private Roman Catholic school and had cut my teeth as a low-key lawyer in New Jersey. I had seen The Trump Organization up close already, and it was exciting, unlike any place I'd ever worked. But seeing it wasn't the same as working there.

Donald Trump had been primarily a New York developer with some other projects in Atlantic City and Las Vegas. Now he was suddenly looking at opportunities in England, Ireland, France, Greece, Egypt, India, Indonesia, and elsewhere. We were all looking at the future of the business going international. The United States would always be our home, but we had many eyes on foreign jurisdictions.

This was the golden era of The Trump Organization.

As the business developed, so did the family's input. One by one, three of the Trump children emerged out of the shadows and found their voice and role in the office—first Don Jr., then Ivanka, and finally Eric. Their impact and learning curve was swift, as they were given projects to launch and licensing deals to develop, and they began to help the Trump Org continue to ride the crest of the wave.

As with many other businessmen, Donald J. Trump had built his empire on long hours, ingenuity, and a significant amount of debt to help fund the increasingly ambitious developments that he wanted to create across the New York skyline. Now, flush with television money and international licensing deals, he was determined to establish a deeper foundation that was based on equity. He drilled his new mantra into everyone: "We're not going to take any debt. We're going to do this with cash."

Previously he had been known as the king of debt and leverage deals. He was now entering a period when he was getting significant income from *The Apprentice*, product licensing, real estate licensing deals, books, speaking engagements, and property operations. I remember he once said to me, "Why should I take the risk of putting up a ninety-story building when I can do one season of *The Apprentice* and make tens of millions?"

In that period, the ninety-story Trump World Tower (TWT) at United Nations Plaza sold out, and he had great success with other buildings such as those in Las Vegas and Chicago. It was a perfect storm of cash, and it created the foundation to do a lot of the equity deals that occurred over the more than a decade I have worked with him since.

That's not saying that he became 100 percent debt-free. Having a balanced level of debt is a healthy thing. However, he wasn't overextended anymore. He had both cash and debts, and therefore, he had a very firm foundation to stand on.

The licensing and real estate deals gained traction for Trump. He lent his name to hotels and other property deals and provided assistance during their construction, as well as marketing and management help. As a consequence, the Trump Org was given significant up-front fees and pieces of the profit as the money flowed in.

Trump had previously handled most of the effort: going out to find and purchase land, working through the approval process, and then putting up a building—so these licensing deals were great. There was no money required up front, and it was all liquid at the outset without the risk.

It also came at a time when Trump was backing off some

US-based investments because the real estate market was beginning to get very hot and expensive. Trump could smell danger brewing as investors threw too much money at overpriced plots of land with easy capital and bundles of debt products in the hope of making a quick buck; what they soon faced was one of the biggest financial crashes our nation, and the rest of the globe, had ever seen.

Trump wanted to diversify his portfolio and look at capitalizing on the licensing projects coming his way. He of course looked at doing deals in every jurisdiction outside the United States to spread his risk and take advantage of better opportunities elsewhere, the same way that other real estate developers looked at new and emerging markets. However, while The Trump Organization would always look at things, there's a big difference between looking at a deal and actually moving forward with it—there's a lot of steps in between, and deals in many geographic areas never came to pass.

Trump was now a global player, and everyone wanted to bask in that reflected glory and get into the name. However, he never strayed from the plan.

Heading into that building that day, I realized it was possibly the most prestigious address in Manhattan. The days ahead would never be dull; there was always a wide variety of people coming through those big doors and taking the gold elevator to the twenty-sixth floor. Visitors came from the political and sporting worlds, entertainers and regular Americans who had ideas to discuss with him and business to pitch. On any given day, you could meet Neil Young, Leonardo DiCaprio, Shaquille O'Neal, P. Diddy, or politicians from across the world. All of them wanted to discuss their ideas, share their thoughts, or come in and say hello to Trump—and he welcomed them all.

Just five minutes in his office showed the real Donald J. Trump, and it was inevitably not what anyone had been led to expect. It was rarely awkward—he can get along well with almost anyone. He can fit into many different situations in a way few other people can. It's one of the skills that make him unique. I participated in the hiring of numerous people over the years, and I always found it surprising to see how a prospective employee would react to him. The vast majority of those who passed through the doors left with the feeling, *Wow, he's a really great guy.*

When you walk onto the twenty-sixth floor of Trump Tower, you come out of what can only be described as a pretty sumptuous elevator and into a very comfortable environment. It's like 1980s luxury but in a tasteful way. It's not at all over the top, as you might expect. I've been in plenty of offices in Manhattan that you could say were much more ostentatious, and the twenty-sixth floor, back then, was really calm, comfortable, and user friendly. When DJT wanted someone, he would shout from behind his desk for that person to come to him. His secretaries would go and get the individual; there was an old-fashioned charm to it.

He didn't use email himself; he liked to have them printed out and read them, and either dictated a response, or, more usually, wrote his thoughts on the printout and sent it back the way it had come. It was a two-way street. If I read something or noticed something, I would write a note and send it to him, and he would always respond. He either liked it, didn't like it, or he wanted to talk about it. Simple but effective communication. A real personal touch, which seems lost in our current world.

He was very focused on the right way to do things; there were no short, sharp emails. He wanted proper communication: conversation or letters. He knew that you got far more out of face-to-face conversation than an impersonal email with no inflection, sense of mood, or tone.

The Trump Organization was such an exciting place because of the steady flow of information in and out. It wasn't a formal environment. You got feedback regularly and every day. We didn't sit alone in our offices typing away, with only our annual review to tell us how things were going. You always knew where you stood, sometimes good and sometimes bad. I suppose to some people that might feel like chaos, but I'd call it caring deeply about your colleagues and your work.

Many times during our projects, especially those overseas, issues would arise that would require me to contact Trump very early in the morning—because of the time zone—and he once told me, "You can call me in my home any time after five a.m." I never hesitated to call his apartment whenever I felt the need to. For the record, when you call his residence, he answers the phone himself—or Melania does—even that early in the morning.

For him and his whole senior team, the work wasn't a job as much as a lifestyle. Silicon Valley sometimes pretends that it invented loving your job and being available whenever the business needs it. Not quite. Even though Trump has respect for personal boundaries—I always felt that when work was done, we were on our own time—like most high-performing CEOs, he still hoped to find you available.

Throughout my time at Trump Tower, there were occasions when I thought the day was over and I'd get a phone call or a knock on my door and be asked to come back and discuss something. However, when you enjoy what you're doing, these things really aren't burdens.

This is a book about that time. It's about a key decade that defined a man who became our most unconventional president. It's the story of how a CEO pivoted his business to make hundreds of millions of dollars, and then gave it all up to serve his country for free.

Trump has always been fascinating to the media, so it's been strange to see so many books published by men who barely know him. Each of these books is written as if Donald Trump fell from the sky in 2015, instead of descending an escalator in a building he made famous with a long-running hit television show. These accounts miss so much about the man. They pile questions on top of mysteries on top of mistaken assumptions, all of which have easy answers in the past.

This book gives the whole picture of a complicated, brilliant man, a man of contradictions. Sometimes he's unshakable in his opinions, and the rest of the time he wants to know what every person he meets thinks he should do. He can angrily insult someone and consider it water under the bridge the next day. He loves hot dogs and Diet Coke, but has more energy than the healthiest eaters I know. He's mastered Twitter, but prefers talking in person to anything technology can offer. He gives tremendous responsibility to talented but relative neophytes. However, he never loses track of the details. He loves consulting with experts, but he's just as interested in what his waitress or a random fan thinks. He went from being the king of debt to a constant seeker of good investments. He loves putting his name on buildings, but he's always willing to give credit to others when it's due.

As we'll see from the stories in this book, complicated as he is, he's defined by one question: What do the customers want? He never stops asking what viewers, citizens, golfers, vacationers, or tenants hope to see and hear today. His famous tirades are always aimed at someone doing something he's sure his customers won't like. His greatest scorn is for people who think about what is necessary, not what's possible.

He's taken that concern from the boardroom to the campaign trail to the White House. He wants an Afghanistan policy that impresses a marine more than it impresses the generals. He wants a trade policy that helps out steel mill workers, regardless of what economists advise. When he's talking about the swamp, he's talking about an army of know-it-alls who have lost touch with the citizens they went to Washington to serve.

He's happy to delegate any project, no matter how important, to someone he trusts. But when he knows what needs to be done, he's happy to make it happen himself.

I remember when we were at Turnberry, our historic golf course and hotel complex in South Ayrshire, Scotland. After a long day at work, several members of our team, including Trump's son Eric, were sitting downstairs in the hotel lounge thinking that the day was over. At about eleven o'clock, in came Trump, full of energy and enthusiasm, wanting to hang paintings that we had brought with us to the hotel. They'd been crated up and brought over, and DJT—as everyone in the organization knows him—was eager to get them open and put them up, to add the Trump touch to this new property in the empire. He was so excited at the prospect of doing this that he was like a kid at Christmas. So, despite the fact we'd all had a long day and were utterly exhausted, we all hopped up and wandered off to see where the pictures and paintings should be hung. For the next two hours, all of us, including Eric, walked around the hotel hanging those photos and paintings. It must have been hilarious to watch. There were two of his senior executives—one of them his own son—standing with these massive picture frames up against the wall, and DJT looking at them from every angle to judge whether they were in the right place, at the right height and whether they looked appropriate in the spot. We'd spend several arm-aching minutes making sure they were hanging perfectly, as dictated by the boss, and then we'd move on to the next one. This didn't happen just once, either; I remember doing the same thing at Doral, this time without Eric—and it was so much harder on my own!

You can imagine the look on the faces of golfers, vacationers, and staff members as they saw this global celebrity wandering through the hotel corridors with an entourage of people hanging paintings and directing their location and deciding whether they were straight or crooked. People just couldn't believe that he would be personally involved in a seemingly trivial task, but it was something that he loved doing. They all stopped and stared at this amazing sight as if it were some kind of ploy for TV.

For DJT, it was no stunt. He was focused on getting the details just right.

Don Jr., Ivanka, and Eric were directly involved in the business. They're equally hardworking, grounded, and down-to-earth, like their father. Children are a reflection of their parents, and I have to say, Donald has done a great job with them. I have a solid relationship with all the siblings, and in all the interactions I've had with them I've never felt that I wasn't a part of the family; I have always been treated as an equal. Sure, we've had our fights and arguments, but we always believed we were in it together. Often there would be a big blowout, and everyone would air his or her views; then we'd get a decision and move on. There were never any grudges held. It was passionate and exciting, and from hearing all the views, we'd arrive at the right decision.

Their father made his children work, and on many occasions he was even harder on them than he was with the rest of the team—they didn't have a free pass by any stretch of the imagination. There are many tragic examples of classic rich kids whose lives go awry, but all of Mr. Trump's children are a positive reflection of their father and are respected by the entire company.

It couldn't have been any other way. Trump was driven and passionate, and he expected the best from everyone. He was the hardest-working guy at the company; everyone knew it, and no one disputed it. Most of the time, he merely worked through his lunch with whatever the entrée of the day was at the downstairs Trump buffet. I was once sitting in his office, and he was eating meatloaf from the cafeteria downstairs. He looked up and said, "People think I'm going to lunch at Le Cirque every day! However, I'm sitting here at my desk working with you!" He laughed about it.

How much is he worth? Well, to be frank, I have absolutely no idea and even less interest in finding out.

His net worth was never of much interest to us. Sure, I was aware of the potential profitability of the projects I was directly involved in, but there were myriad developments occurring all the time, and money raised from one would be reinvested in another. For DJT, it was never really about the cash he put into the bank, but more the excitement of the projects he created—and there's no doubt he created a significant portfolio of amazing properties, golf courses, and real estate developments that made him asset rich. To DJT, it was creating things that drove him on, not the money he made—that was just a necessity to keep building and moving forward.

There will always be those who are jealous or who decry what he's done, but this is a man who started in real estate and went on to become one of only forty-four people in the history of planet earth to lead its greatest nation.

Whatever you think of him, you can't dispute that.

CHAPTER 2

Sealing the Deal with Trump

G rowing up as a kid in New Jersey, I knew Trump as a larger-than-life, legendary character who flitted through the social and business pages of the New York newspapers. I vividly remember reading openmouthed all about him as he opened the Taj Mahal casino in Atlantic City—then the biggest of its kind in the world. No one on the planet was doing what Mr. Trump was doing, and there in Atlantic City, he was beating the casino big boys at their own game. This man was known as a winner and a brash, pugnacious entrepreneur who didn't take no for an answer.

What stood out for me, aside from his real estate projects, were the colossal boxing matches he held in the 1980s and '90s, when Mike Tyson was the champ. That was my view of him: a mysterious, brilliant real estate developer and casino operator who exuded not just luxury but ultraluxury. Media exposure was in his blood, and he seemed to revel in the notoriety that came with it, long before *The Apprentice* hit our screens and made him an even bigger celebrity. Just imagine what he'd have made of Twitter if it had been available back then.

Had Trump transcended the national consciousness? For a kid growing up in New Jersey, I thought he certainly had. He had it all: glamour, success, and the trappings of a great life, as well as appearing bold and thriving alongside formidable women in the social diary pages of the *New York Post* and the *Daily News*. It was certainly a world away from my own background. I was never interested in fame, and I never pictured myself working for a celebrity. But Trump, and The Trump Organization, is so much more than that.

My father was a handsome Egyptian surgeon—a Coptic Orthodox Christian—who'd fled religious discrimination in his homeland, and my mother a beautiful Scottish nurse. They'd moved to New Jersey from the United Kingdom when I was a few years old. I stayed far from the world Trump inhabited, moving to Manhattan only in 1998 after I'd graduated from the JD/MBA program at Boston University, unsure of my path in life. I spent another two years doing my postdoctoral law degree (LLM) at night while working for the government, spending days in civil commitment court proceedings and often dealing with violent sex offenders and very sick psychiatric patients. Reading the case files and having to deal with this unfortunate aspect of humanity was not pleasant; I saw the darkest side of life and knew I had to get out before it consumed me.

The best way to get to know New York is to get out and walk around. I would wake up on Saturday and pick a random direction and begin walking with no particular target in mind or view of how far I'd get. One time, I went to First Avenue and walked by the United Nations—I always thought it was an extraordinary place, especially as my family is from Egypt and Scotland. I stumbled across a nearby building under construction, and there was a huge billboard with a picture of him. Trump World Tower, with ninety stories of residences, was being heralded as the tallest residential building in the world. I stood on the steps and looked at the frame of this megastructure thinking, *Who will live in this incredible building?* It was just so unimaginable for me, and I had a moment when I thought that to live in a DJT building would be unreal.

So, fast-forward a few years, to mid-2002, and I was in private practice working alongside my great friend Paul Werther in New Jersey. We were representing a group of successful Wall Street executives who had purchased the former estate of the discredited car engineer and manufacturer John DeLorean from the bankruptcy court with the intention of turning it into a golf complex. They had envisioned the massive 484-acre former DeLorean estate in Bedminster as a golf course and high-end housing project with membership fees in the high six figures before the banks foreclosed on mortgages worth several million dollars.

At the time, the real estate market was surging, and lots of people plowed into it not knowing what they were do- ing but thinking they could make an awful lot of money. Of course, it's never that easy, and many people have been burned thinking they could become real estate developers. Before our involvement, the Wall Street guys had contracted with a supposed golf course development company, but after a couple of years of frustration and inaction and millions of dollars spent, there wasn't much to show for their money. One of the leaders of the group, Ashley Cooper, who would later become a senior executive with The Trump Organiza- tion, asked Paul for help getting rid of the development com- pany, and Paul and the team managed to do it—but it wasn't easy. Ashley had done a fantastic job of nailing down the acquisition and getting the project rolling, but was moving on toward different things.

Now, Paul and Ashley were searching for the people who could turn the dream into a reality—or the investment would be a total bust—and they set about finding someone to take over the Bedminster project. There were a couple of big names in golf who looked at it and couldn't make the deal. Paul was in New York, and he called me up, and it was just surreal as he began whispering down the phone saying he was in Trump's office and that he was likely to buy this thing. It was a bizarre moment. DJT's decision to buy the project was made relatively quickly, but it wasn't something that was going to come easily. Nothing involving Trump ever is—you have to scrap for every part of the deal. He is the ultimate negotiator, of course.

We spent only a month on this incredible deal.

Trump's chief lawyer was Jason Greenblatt, who lived out in New Jersey near where our office was. We gave him a conference room, and he moved in for a month while we worked around the clock, first negotiating the terms of the contract of sale, poring over every clause, every sentence, every element of it, and then going through due diligence before finally closing the deal. We spent days on that project, calling in for pizza as we worked long into the night to get all the elements of the contract resolved. It was typical Trump: very fast, messy, a lot of moving parts on the table, but in the end, the transaction closed. Trump was happy, and our clients were satisfied as well.

It was around this time that Trump was also looking to push into Chicago with the building of his Trump International Hotel and Tower, so he certainly had his hands full!

During the Bedminster process, we became very friendly with Jason and the other members of the team; it sometimes happens that way. Transactional work is not like litigation, where you're trying to win; rather, winning is closing, and everyone is in the same boat, working toward similar goals. We wanted to come out of this with a deal that suited all parties, but we also all wanted to feel like we'd gotten a good deal, too. That's not often the outcome of these kinds of negotiations. It was in this case, however.

That was my first experience of The Trump Organization.

The deal was done by a small group of people very quickly, one of the fastest deals I'd ever done. I've since done lots that were even faster, but at the time this was a game-changing experience for me. To work alongside an organization like that and deal with someone I'd admired for years was just incredible. We'd have conference calls with Jason, and Trump would come on the phone.

When I was growing up, I wasn't exposed to celebrities or any people you saw on TV. I lived a relatively quiet life, almost in a proverbial bubble of just friends and close family. I'd walked into Paul's office, and I heard this booming voice on the other end of the squawk box. It was an eminently recognizable voice, even for someone so sheltered as I had been.

What struck everyone during those series of calls—when Trump and Paul did most of the speaking—was that this was a real hands-on guy leading his team in the negotiation with us. He was first on the issues. He knew what he was talking about, from the strategic overview to the smallest detail. That's what grabbed me the most: just how much he knew about what he was talking about. I guess I had expected him to have handed over all of this kind of work to underlings, while he spent his time rubbing elbows with celebrities and checking on just the headline issues. However, here was the man who was negotiating the deal, involved in the details. I found him to be approachable and calm; he knew his position and was advocating strongly for it. He wasn't belligerent, and he didn't talk down to us. There was an awful lot of give and take.

Part of the negotiations meant that the sixty or so people who had already paid tens of thousands of dollars each to be original members under the previous regime were set to lose everything. However, Trump didn't turn them over as he could have, and he certainly didn't trample them in the dirt. He honored their memberships and allowed them to remain as founding members of the new Trump National Golf Club

Bedminster. By ditching them—as he had every legal right to do—he could have saved himself millions of dollars. However, he was shrewd and smart about it, too; he knew that this was sixty or so people whom he had on the books, happy and grateful from the get-go, and that they would be with him and paying their annual dues for a long time. He was the absolute opposite of a bully—and those people were thrilled at becoming founding members of what would become one of New Jersey's best golf courses.

When he met those members, he was confident, of course, but he was also very polite. I can tell you now, he's very respectful of the people on the other side of the table. Of course, he knows that he has an aura, and Trump uses that advantage when he walks in the room to try to get what he wants. Hey, that's business. It was a negotiation process that was two sided: we got something, and he got something. Everyone was happy, and it's now a great club that hosts top tournaments, and many of those founding members are still there.

Shortly after closing, it came time for the ground-breaking, and I was invited. I was one of only about 150 people in total, and I was amazed to find Trump in attendance. I stood a few feet from him and Melania in the clubhouse.

It was not what I was expecting to see; if, indeed, I had assumed anything before. It's the only time in my life that I've seen him wearing jeans. Other than his trademark suits, I think I've only ever seen him in golf gear or black tie. However, there he was in jeans, a buttoned-down collared shirt, and a blazer, and I remember him wearing some form of cowboy boots. It certainly wasn't trademark Trump.

He was getting shrimp, and I thought, *When will I get the opportunity to speak to him ever again?* I walked over and introduced myself. I didn't feel nervous. He was very complimentary about Paul and excited about the Bedminster deal that had been thrashed out, and how he was going to build a great golf course and club.

I said, "I've heard that your mother was born in Scotland, is that true?" (Remember, this was in the earliest days of Wikipedia, before it was easy to go online and check stuff like this.)

Well, it turned out that his mother and my mom were both born in the same small town of Stornoway on a small island off the west coast of Scotland and home to only about eight thousand people. The coincidence was very fortuitous for me. I could tell his attention perked up a notch when he fired back, "What do you know about Stornoway?"

The tone of the discussion changed straightaway. He'd been engaged and polite, but suddenly this was something completely different; he'd found a common theme. We were just two guys talking about my twenty years of summer holidays on that idyllic isle, and how different that world was from the one we now both inhabited.

I told him I was living on the Upper East Side, was renting, and was looking to buy something, and he said, "I have a new building, Trump World Tower, we're just finishing it now and I want you in the building." Just like that. *I want you in the building.* No request, no questions: *I want you in the building.* He told me to call Jason on Monday, and he'd give me the name of the person to get me in there. I thanked him for everything, and I remember telling everyone I'd met him.

When I first saw him there was a certain aura about

him; he has such a commanding presence that cuts across generations—whether it's a young child or someone from my parents' generation, it has an impact on everyone. My young son recently met him, gave him a fist bump, and he still talks about it all the time. Even if you don't know who he is, you know by the way he carries himself he has power and influence.

In person, he's very polite, soft spoken, and interested in making you comfortable right away. He does the little things right: he'll ask, "Would you like a drink?" "How is your family?" or "How have you been?" He never makes you feel like it's a privilege to talk to him; in actuality, he's very courteous and thanks you for coming to see him. It's a sign of the little old-world charm that unfortunately gets tossed aside in today's all-business mentality. He is very engaged and focused and not like other stars who blow you off.

I contacted Jason on Monday, and I went there with my broker Dennis Mangone and looked at the building and was blown away by it. Until that point I'd spent two years looking at apartments across the city and had never found anything that I liked. This was beautiful, livable, and in a location I was comfortable with, and I could find a unit in my price zone.

I was impressed when I made the deal that my name was on the deed as the buyer and Trump's was on it as the seller. He told me when we made the deal, "Look, people love living in my buildings. You're gonna really love it. I have lots of my friends live in the building—and they all love it."

When I closed on the unit, I had only $2,000 left to my name, and people thought I was crazy. However, my father was behind me and understood. I'd invested everything I had, but I knew it wasn't wrong. I would enjoy it, live in it, and when the time was right would have a healthy investment.

Trump World Tower, directly across the street from the United Nations building on First Avenue, was not located in an area you would think about when you had your sights set on a luxury apartment, and certainly not one on the scale that Trump was thinking about when he started building it in the late 1990s. However, DJT helped transform that area, selling units in his building to diplomats and many wealthy people, and he broke convention as to where to locate this kind of high-rise, making a lot of money along the way.

He defies convention, and he challenges the concerns and fears of others.

On the day I moved into the building, I remembered the day when I'd stood on the steps and watched it under construction. As I turned the key and wandered into the big, open space with no furniture, I reminisced about the question I'd asked myself that day, gazing up at the magnificent building. I replied to myself almost in a hush, "I guess I'm the kind of guy who lives in an apartment like this."

CHAPTER 3

The Lure of
Fifth Avenue

Buying an apartment in Trump World Tower wasn't the end of my interactions with the Trump Org, or DJT, for that matter. Quite the contrary: it was just the merest hint of what was still to come—and the beginning, unbeknownst to me, of a long and fruitful career with Donald J. Trump.

Paul Werther and I continued to interact and work with the organization, including the finance and acquisition of what would become Trump Plaza Jersey City, so the relationship continued.

And I loved living in the awesome place that was Trump World Tower.

As we've all seen, DJT has a habit of spending time at his properties, so I would see him at the annual meeting of the unit owners. He would always come and take part. Then there was the annual holiday party, which would occur in mid-December and would be held in the lobby, and 90 percent of the residents would be there. Trump would come by, speak to everyone, say a few words, and make jokes. He was great with everyone.

Trump World Tower was filled with athletes, musicians, and movie stars, household names and prominent business leaders. It was an excellent place to live, and people would sell and buy bigger units in the building. You didn't leave; it was an extraordinary building. No one seemed to want to go, from staff to owners. It was beautiful and well run, which isn't necessarily the case in Manhattan. It was precisely what the Trump brand represented, and there was a solid sense of community and family all wrapped up in a ninety-story building. Everyone knew each other.

One day in the fall of 2005, I was working at my law firm when I had a call from Trump's secretary, the wonderful Rhona Graff. She asked if I could come and see him immediately. I suppose it was unusual to get the call, but it wasn't a total surprise. I dropped everything without question and immediately went to his office. I drove over there in about ten minutes flat, as the roads, for a change, were completely clear. I dropped the car off at Trump World Tower and walked over having no idea of what he wanted, other than that he'd like to see me. I wasn't nervous, as I had tremendous respect for him. As far as I was concerned, he was down-to-earth, no BS, and he treated me with respect, too.

I was curious. What was I being asked to come over about?

I'd walked by Trump Tower, on Fifth Avenue and Fifty-Seventh Street, thousands of times. That's the center of life for New Yorkers. I'd been in there a dozen times or more, to grab a coffee and a bite to eat or to use the restroom. However, this time it was different. I was here to see the man.

I went up to the security guard in front of the big gold elevator and told him about my meeting with Mr. Trump. Of course, they didn't send me straight up, but rang first to check my credentials, and then I was on my way.

I was thinking, *What the hell has this guy got for me?* I was rolling over in my mind that call: *Can you come to his office right now?* Not tomorrow, but right now.

I came off the elevator, and funnily enough, it was what I expected: tremendously plush in a 1980s way with a fantastic view of Central Park. I took a seat and started to flip through a magazine as I waited. Before long, I heard his voice booming in the background, and he came out of his office to greet me before we sauntered back in to chat. I didn't even notice the office that first time, as I was so taken aback by him coming out to greet me, rather than have me sent in, and by our subsequent discussion.

After the basic common courtesies, he asked me if I knew about an issue that was going on in the building in Trump World Tower. I said I was aware of it and we discussed it for a while before he introduced me to other people in his office. I didn't even take my topcoat off. I wasn't overwhelmed, but I was drawn into our one-on-one substantive conversation.

He was asking my opinion about TWT issues, and I later saw how often he sought the advice of all kinds of people. I never felt that I couldn't give an opinion. He might not accept a person's view, but he certainly does listen. It's a valuable lesson: take many views and hear multiple opinions, they can illuminate a situation differently.

We talked about the issue, and he asked if I could get a few people together to resolve it, and since I agreed and felt very strongly that he was right, it represented an opportunity on many levels. It was an opportunity to take an active role in the most critical investment in my life and an opportunity for me to work more closely with him and his organization. Michael Cohen, later to become the infamous counsel to the Trump Org—and, well, we all know the rest—was introduced to me, and we put a group together and took a leadership position on the board of TWT. I became the president of that board, and on an ongoing and regular basis, I was in and out of The Trump Organization. TWT was a complicated building, with three-hundred-plus units, so there were issues about the budget, maintenance, staff, and the like, and I began to interact with people in the organization.

Pretty soon, I'd met Don Jr., Ivanka, and Eric.

The first time I met Eric and Ivanka, it was around the fall of 2006, and I was coming in to discuss a TWT matter with DJT. I entered his office, and he had all the architectural drawings and renderings for a project to build a golf development in Aberdeen, Scotland, laid out on his desk. Don Jr., Ivanka, and Eric were discussing the plans, and I was lucky enough to get a first look. I have always been impressed that Trump uses real terms of endearment with the kids, the same terms of affection I use with my children. He looks out for those kids, and is focused on two things: he wants them to learn, but he also wants to protect them. He brought his kids in to work in the company and entrusted them with responsibility and leadership positions. He'd give them guidance and help.

They asked for my opinion on things, and they made me feel incredibly welcome. There wasn't a hint of pretension, and although, outwardly, it would seem an intimidating environment to be in, I was incredibly comfortable with everyone, and I was grateful to have the access and the chance to look at a plan like that. I could tell it was a project that was very special to Trump, and little did I know that six months later he would entrust me to take a leading role in its development.

My first meeting with Don Jr. took place much earlier, at another ground-breaking, this time for the Jersey City building (another Paul Werther client). I was standing with five or six people chatting about nothing for twenty minutes. I realized that I didn't know who I'd been talking to, and so introduced myself and he revealed himself to be Donald Trump Jr. He, too, was down-to-earth and easy to get along with, despite the fact he was just out of his twenties. *You know what?* I started to think, *I'd like to work with these guys.*

I had those discussions with Bernie Diamond—he was co-general counsel alongside Jason—and we spoke about this for several months, and he eventually said, "Do you want me to mention this to Mr. Trump?" and I said if it could be done quietly, sure.

Then one day I was in Trump's office dealing with some

other issue with TWT, and he said, "Bernie tells me that you're interested in working for the organization, so let me have your résumé." From then on, we went through a period where he would ask me to look at things. One of them was to look at SEC filings for his casinos. Now, I'm no expert in this, and so I called a great friend of mine, Scott Goodman, who is an SEC expert at Day Pitney, one of my former law firms, and we spent the whole weekend going through the public company filings, literally huddled over them in my apartment.

A week or so went by, and I went to talk to DJT about a few things, and he brought up the filings and asked me a question: "You looked at my SEC filings—what do you think is the one best thing that I got out of the deal I made at Atlantic City?"

We chatted about the deal for forty-five minutes and discussed how deals of this nature are structured, and I was impressed with his grasp of some very complex issues. You never think guys of his caliber are very involved, but as I got to know him, that's what impressed me most: he looks at every different angle. I was amazed that he remembered what we were dealing with and would send us interesting documents when he was working in these spheres.

The bottom line is, he asked me if I was happy where I was at my firm, and I told him I was fine but that if he was asking if I was passionate, then the truth was that I'd always been inspired about property and real estate.

My father's brother, whom I was named after, had a tremendous impact on me. He was a military contractor, to begin with, and he built airports and many other projects across the Middle East and then went on to focus on charitable work for the church and low-income families. I'd also worked in plumbing for Cofone Plumbing and Heating during high school and college. Lou Cofone, whose business it was, had a significant influence on me, and I learned such a tremendous amount from him. I told Trump I didn't want to spend my life papering deals, I wanted to build things. He said, "I want you on board, but this can't happen unless Paul says it's okay. He's a good guy to do business with, and I don't want to offend him if he thinks he can't afford to lose you."

We discussed it for a good while, and despite the fact my future career hung in the balance somewhat, I was impressed at how serious he was and how important it was for him not to damage his relationship with Paul. I'm not easily dumbstruck, but this was an occasion when DJT had me lost for words—and in a good way. I was never worried about it, because Paul had my best interests at heart, but I was impressed that Trump would seek approval from anybody. In the cutthroat world of New York real estate development, who does that? It's a dog-eat-dog mentality, with people taking what they can get, irrespective of the impact it may have on either themselves or the competition—that's just life. It happens in every business, everywhere across the world.

In retrospect, I have great admiration for and understanding of why Trump did it. I think it was a combination of respect for Paul and an astute assessment that you never know when a casual contact may become a significant opportunity. However, it was even more than that—it was just the right thing to do. And as I came to know while working for The Trump Organization, DJT had a particular soft spot for Paul and for people who worked alongside him. Trump appreciated the time Paul had invested in people and how much he'd spent coaching and developing his team, and Trump didn't feel it was right that other companies would poach Paul's employees without even the faintest hint of gratitude or appreciation. His primary motivation was that seeking such approval was the right thing to do. It's just another example of the kind of operator he is. Despite how he's often portrayed, he's just an old-school guy.

You'd never read about that in the *Washington Post* or the *New York Times* or amid the usual fire-and-brimstone fairy tales that you might see elsewhere, because they seem intent only to make Trump out to be a monster and someone cavalier with other people's emotions and feelings.

I know differently.

Paul later told me that after we closed the deal and DJT became the owner of the Bedminster property, he called Paul a couple of weeks later and said, "George is a great guy who did some great work," and then he asked Paul if he'd mind if he went ahead and hired me.

"I, of course, said that I would never stand in the way of George's progress and if it were good for his career then he would have my blessing," Paul said. It didn't surprise him, because he'd known Trump for years.

Paul admits they'd all had concerns about doing the Bedminster deal because of Trump's reputation for how he went about business. However, the reason Paul believes they managed to close the deal was that Trump was beyond a gentleman, beyond open, and beyond fair. "He wanted to get a great deal, sure, but he was so open and clear in what he wanted," Paul said. "He would call up and chat about land costs and ask opinions about things, and we knew exactly where we stood. I played golf with him a couple of times, and he was a great guy, so I wasn't surprised when he called me up and said, 'Would you have a problem if I hire George?' "

I saw this scenario repeat itself many times, when DJT or his other executives would seek approval from another business leader before they employed a chosen candidate.

Tell me where else this happens these days?

I was hired.

CHAPTER 4

To the Land of
My Ancestors

The Trump Organization offered me the job at the end
of the summer of 2006, and I didn't know what the
job was. DJT believed there was a talent to be nurtured, but as is the way of things in the company, there wasn't
a ready-made role for me to slot into. If that sounds like a
remarkable way to hire people, that's because it is. Trump
never knew when a future opportunity might arise, and he
liked to have people he'd trained and trusted ready and waiting. He hates to see talent wasted.

We agreed I would start full time in January, but the plan

was that I would come in from time to time in the interim to acquire some background and to get to know people. In the fall of 2006, I was in and out of there as much as I could, not formally working, but meeting people and just trying to figure out where I fit in. Trump knew I didn't want to practice law, so he said, "Let's get you in, and we'll find out where you fit and thrive."

Being able to recognize talent and determine where people's skills fit is utterly critical. If you look at skilled artisans with raw talent, you can see that they know what tool to use to produce something correctly. Knowing which guy is going to get the job done is the difference between success and failure. For DJT, it was simple. "I'll find the right place for you," he said, and I trusted that he would.

Also, I wasn't the only one in the company whom he sought to help in that way.

Sometime during those last few weeks of 2006, I went to the Christmas holiday party, which used to be held in the Rainbow Room above the Rockefeller Center. I couldn't believe I was there. I had a grin from ear to ear that lasted for weeks. There were maybe five or six hundred people in the room—Trump was there, along with a bunch of people in the organization whom I had gotten to know as the president of the board of TWT. Also, it was on that very night that I met my future wife, who worked for the organization. There was so much food and drink, and people were having a great time.

Trump also had an annual tradition in which the names of all the employees would be written on pieces of paper and put in a box, and then he'd hold a drawing. There were TVs,

CDs, and all sorts of prizes. And then there would be cash to be won. "Okay, we're going to give away $1,000"—and he'd pull a name from the box. Then the prize would go to $5,000, $10,000, and finally end at $15,000. That year, he was having so much fun that he pulled one name out, looked at it, and then threw the piece of paper on the floor and said, "Well, he's not getting the money! He's cost me too much already." And, yes, he was only kidding—the staff member still got the money and there was a lot of laughter.

The whole atmosphere was just fabulous, and it created a wonderful family feeling.

After I'd started working full time in the organization, Trump called me into his office at the end of February 2007 and asked if I would like to be in charge of his project in Scotland.

I was shocked. What did I know about golf?

I told him that I don't know the rules, and that I didn't even like the game—things have changed since, but at that time, one of the most painful things for me was to sit down and watch golf on TV. It was the most boring thing in the world. He said, "Even better, you'll learn.

"I want you to study everything that's been done so far, and I really want to get the application in. You need to go over right away—this weekend—and spend the whole of the next week there. There are environmental issues, and the team is saying we can't do anything about it."

He was adamant it needed sorting now.

He said, "Go see the people, and if you find any problems with the team, get rid of them, because if we're having issues now, they will only get worse as you move forward. Spend the first few days walking up and down that site, walk every inch of it, meet the people and find out the issues. But I want it [the planning application] in this year, I want it approved this year, and I want to start building it in January 2008."

So that was it—there were no other comments other than to get it done. Trump believes people are at their best when they're in a bit over their heads.

I'm pretty confident in general, but even I was thinking, *Holy shit!*

He said, "Your mother is from Scotland, my mother is from Scotland, and we're going to build a great development. You will really enjoy this and have fun doing it."

It's different now, and I enjoy nothing more than building some of the world's best golf courses, playing on them, and watching golf on TV. But at the time, Trump had just told me to get on a flight and head over that week to meet the people, learn the project, and have fun. I really couldn't get my head around it. Before I knew it, I had a ticket in my hand, and I'd been empowered to meet the team and make any decisions I wanted.

Now, Trump is very involved, he likes attention to detail, but he's not a micromanager. He wants a result. If there are bumps in the road, he doesn't care as long as you know what the result he wants is. He cares about what he cares about, and the rest is what he hired you for. There's no hiding there, you have to produce, and if you don't, you have failed. It's a different situation from so many other places of work. Many organizations are process driven, and if you don't get the results, it's okay. It's not like that in The Trump Organization. You get the results, man, or you fail.

However, that's where I wanted to be: under pressure. Extreme pressure can either break you or create a diamond. The thrill of leadership and doing my own thing was incredible, and the love for this project and the country of my ancestors made me so happy. Trump said, "You've got to love what you do or you're never going to be happy." I was intimidated by the challenge, but I was so psyched that I'd been given this incredible opportunity. I planned to learn everything I could about it, from every angle, and I would figure out how to succeed.

It was the beginning of a massive project that changed my life. It's also one that reveals a lot about the man who owned it.

Scotland was my ancestral home, where I'd spent six weeks a year in my formative years running wild in Stornoway on the island of Lewis, fishing and hunting and crofting (my family had sheep and cows). I walked out of there and called my dad and said it was unbelievable that I'd been told I was in charge of this enormous project worth hundreds of millions of dollars, to build golf courses, hotels, and homes.

Trump had done what he promised he'd do: he'd found the right place for my talents to shine. And I wasn't the only one he did this for in the company. This is how he did business. Amanda Miller, who started at the Trump Org as a waitress during her summer vacations at Westchester, has never forgotten the efforts DJT made for her and others coming through the ranks who wanted to learn and get involved. Amanda is now senior vice president of marketing and corporate communications and has been with the organization for ten years. You'll have seen her on *The Apprentice*.

Amanda recalled, "Around the time I started here [at

Trump Tower], he asked, 'What about being on the show?' So he asked me to email some details to the producers, and I did eight seasons as the receptionist on the show. It was just fantastic, and all that came about because he knew I was interested in the show when the team was coming and going all the time. All the celebrities that appeared on it would come up and ask me about being an actress and how amazing it must be, but they were shocked when I told them that I worked in marketing for the organization."

For Amanda, it's Trump's talent for helping and supporting his people that marks him out from the crowd. "He has recognized my talent and been so supportive. From my experience, he is incredibly kind and warm. His entire family was at my wedding. . . . He and Melania came. He said, 'We'll stay for cake!' It was so nice. It's very frustrating and annoying when you hear so many negative things said about him or see so many cruel comments written, because he's kind and very fatherly."

That's him: the guy who goes to the team member's wedding, the guy who promotes a young waitress and helps nurture her interest in TV by getting her a role on one of the biggest smash hits on the planet. That's DJT.

And that's what he did for me, too: saw the talent and nurtured it.

Trump is interested in enthusiasm, talent, and results. Experience never mattered as much as those qualities.

CHAPTER 5

Conquer the Unconquerable

D JT gave me the Scotland assignment on a Wednesday. I was blown away and flattered by the chance to show what I could do, so much so that I then spent the next two days in New York trying to learn as much background as possible. The reality of it was that I had no idea what I was going to do.

I didn't know much about the game of golf, and I'd been given the responsibility of overseeing the development of a massive golf resort from scratch. This was not just any golf development and resort, of course, but one that Trump wanted to be the "greatest golf course in the world" and one built as a real tribute to his much-loved mother.

No pressure there, then.

I felt an obligation to say I knew nothing about it. He remained very calm and said, "Don't worry about that. I want you to go over there and look at the plans; it's not so complicated. I want you to learn every inch of the property. Meet the team and see who is good and bad. I want you to have a good time, and enjoy it. It's going to be great."

He also said, "Do the best you can, don't worry about it, and make sure you love it."

After DJT's chat to me about the project, I began to feel slightly more comfortable and was very excited. I hadn't been to Scotland for quite some time, perhaps fourteen or fifteen years. Here was a chance to make my mark, too, on my mother's land. He sent me off, telling me, "I want you to learn everything about the place. Get to know the neighbors and come back with a working knowledge of everything about the project. Meet local people in business, politicians, and see the other amazing courses in Scotland. Then come back and tell me what you find."

There's so much crap written about Trump, but nothing is wider of the mark when it comes to the BS about him being interested in only one thing: money. Yes, it's important to him—who isn't it important to? However, there are sometimes more significant issues at play, and this was one of them.

This was his tribute to the wonderful Mary MacLeod, his mother. He always looked on her very fondly—as well as his sister Maryanne—although she was the one who could tell him what to do! He always said that his mother was a tough cookie. Scotland bred them tough, and there was none tougher than his mother. And as well as being a tribute to his mom, this would ultimately prove to be his legacy, too. This one was personal.

I didn't know much about the history of the sport, or the rules, and I certainly didn't know a thing about what was involved in building a course, let alone one of this magnitude. I had to talk to the experts to immerse myself in the basics of course design and what was required to pull this off.

So it was I found myself talking to the incredible Tommy Fazio, the legendary golf course architect, and he gave me a forty-thousand-foot overview of what was needed. I also did a desktop study speaking to those on the ground in Scotland. And I went out and bought one of the biggest coffee table books ever published on the history of the sport and began to immerse myself in it.

I sat on the flight from Newark to Glasgow thinking, *What the hell am I going to do?*

As I wandered off the flight into the arrivals hall back on my mother's soil, I was met by Lora McCluskey, one of the part-time members of the group who was starting to set things up for DJT. I'd spoken to her before, but you're never quite sure what you're going to get when you arrive. I needn't have worried, because we got on famously immediately.

However, her first question to me was "What do you want me to do?"

I was stumped. I didn't have a clue!

I'd arrived Sunday to get there before I was due to meet the whole development team on Tuesday—I didn't even know whom that development team consisted of! Trump had been clear, though, that I needed to kick-start the application, because he wanted to be building the world's greatest golf course by the end of the year. I wasn't comfortable with labeling a course not even constructed yet as the greatest course in the world, but quietly in my own mind I was thinking, *How can we go to Scotland, the home of golf, and say, "We're building the world's greatest golf course"?*

At some point, I did say, "I don't think we should refer to it in that manner," but Trump just said, "You've got to believe in it and keep saying it because then it will become true. Keep an open mind, set your goals high, and don't take no for an answer." There's a logic to his superlatives.

There were so many people—from advisers to politicians, press to protesters—who kept saying the project was doomed, that it would never see the light of day, and that Trump was wasting his time and money. However, he knew better. No one could persuade him that this wasn't the right thing to do, for him, for the organization, and for the country.

As of this writing, the Trump Org has just announced the next stage of development of that unique golf complex, with five hundred houses, new hotel accommodation, leisure facilities, and retail units. I do not doubt that if not me, then my kids will be watching a British Open Championship there at some point. Where others say no, or "It's just not feasible," Trump can see through the haze, ignore the doubters, and prove them wrong.

Years later, when I'm reflecting, I can understand what he was doing. It was the thinking of a leader, pushing his team forward, even toward an aspirational goal, and changing the entire mind-set of everyone involved. With an initiative like this, giving it such a specific and lofty goal increases morale and generates a sense of pride and ownership for the whole team, who are then all on board and moving in the right direction.

You can see that's how Trump continues to function to this day. It's one of the attributes that sets him aside as a president; there's no lack of leadership when he's on deck. At times you may question his methods, but taking a long view, you can see that he gets results. Look at the tax cuts, NATO, the tariffs, the North Korea meetings, the Supreme Court, and the global trade deals. Surrounded by naysayers, he's kept his promises. How many politicians even try?

He is the master at destabilizing people involved in negotiations, sometimes by raising the stakes so high that he creates panic and chaos, but on the inside, he's calm and laser focused on the objective. That's what you need in a world leader. You don't see him coming, but he knows where he needs to go. People underestimate him at their peril—just ask everyone who went up against him in 2016. That's what makes him different: he's prepared to swim with the sharks. I use these tactics all the time in my day-to-day responsibilities, and they are useful.

During that first trip, I began to get a sense that this wasn't going to be an easy project, because a whole team of experts was saying that I'd never get it approved. What a way to start! The team had gotten so bogged down that they had lost sight of the goal. They weren't properly motivated, and there was almost a self-defeatist attitude among them. My whole group of experts was feeling hopeless before we'd even begun.

I had to get them to know me, earn their trust, and convince them that they could do this. *Yeah, of course we can do this. We have the full weight of The Trump Organization behind us, and we have a track record of achieving what people deem is impossible.* What I also had to do was to get every one of them to believe that yes, we could get this done, or we wouldn't be successful. Set high goals and believe you can accomplish it—and anyone who didn't believe in that mantra was clearly not going to be with us for the whole of the ride. Mr. Trump wouldn't allow that to happen, and so I certainly couldn't. This rested on my shoulders.

It's true that the divide between the United States and the United Kingdom is enormous in terms of personality. Americans are brash and ready to push as hard as we can to get things done, and even if we don't believe something can be achieved, we'll be damned if we admit it! No one wants to be seen as defeatist or unable to aim for the sky. In the United Kingdom, there's not the same chutzpah about projects and certainly not the same gung-ho, go-get-'em approach to getting things done. If there's an obstacle, the British will find it, and often our team got taken down by those hurdles rather than leaping over them. And that's before we even came across the antiquated and parochial Scottish planning system.

The flight came in at seven thirty a.m. Sunday, and I thought it would be good to see some golf courses first before I met the team for our initial meeting on Tuesday. Lora took me to Carnoustie, Kingsbarns, St Andrews—the home of golf; we went to the Old Course Hotel and Swilken Bridge— and I started to realize, as I was being introduced as Donald

Trump's lawyer, that people were treating me very differently, and yes, in an extremely positive way. I felt welcomed and respected, and I said to myself that despite the challenges, I was going to enjoy this. It was interesting, as I'd never been dealt with that way, and the Trump name did open doors. Despite some of the controversy that surrounds him, people know that he's a man who means business. When he says he's going to do something, he gets things done.

Finally, after a long day out on a plethora of amazing golf courses, we meandered our way toward Aberdeen. The roads are pretty limited in that part of the world. There are no major highways like in the United States. From St Andrews to Aberdeen—a distance of just about eighty miles—it took over two hours of driving along country lanes and a two-lane road. The conditions were pretty poor.

It was about six p.m. by the time we arrived, it was March, and the rain was biblical. There was nobody there, no sign of life in MacLeod House—the mansion dating back to the fifteenth century that would eventually become our beautiful hotel but was at this stage nothing more than a run-down shooting lodge—and so I stayed in an old stable block on the site. Then the project manager arrived, a former Scots Guards officer and every inch the former military man. There seemed to be nothing open, and even the local restaurant was closed because it was a Sunday. Can you believe that? I love Scotland, but you couldn't get a meal at the local restaurant because it was a Sunday! There'd be a mutiny in New York if you shut up shop on the weekend.

I was taken to another restaurant about twenty minutes away in the oil city of Aberdeen and then came back to the estate, but it was so dark I couldn't see anything. I kid you not, it was pitch black, and I'm on a 1,400-acre site on my own in the middle of nowhere. I phoned my father, and he said, "Look, go one day at a time and have confidence and faith in yourself. You can handle this, and you know that you can do it. Go in there and do the best you can. Have faith, and trust in God."

He said, "Donald Trump is an experienced guy, and he knows what he's doing, and he wouldn't have picked you if he didn't think you could do this. You're not alone; you have him behind you."

CHAPTER 6

God Has Done All
the Hard Work

The next morning, I could smell the peat on the site, and at MacLeod House, the smell of eggs and bacon was rising out of the old kitchen on the ground floor. It just took me right back to my youth when I'd spent my summers in the wilds of this great country—reassuring smells that comforted me and made me smile. Right there and then, as the smells wafted around me, I knew this would be good for us and good for the people of Scotland. As I savored the tastes of a long-lost childhood, the team began to emerge and congregate in the old, drafty house that had seen better days. There was a vivid red-and-white plaid carpet in the place, and the house needed love and care, but it was a fantastic piece of real estate.

The old baronial mansion was stunning and situated in one of the most amazing locations ever. The wildness of the terrain, those 1,400 acres set among fields, woods, and the most spectacular dune system I'd ever seen, was astounding. Those dunes stretch for something like nineteen miles, along some of the most rugged and beautiful coastline you'll ever see. We hardly touched them during construction. We wanted that to be the centerpiece of the site: the beauty that God created. Even today it takes my breath away.

Previously, the land had been owned by an American lawyer and oil company executive, Tom Griffin, who had used the estate for shooting birds—pheasants, partridge, that sort of thing—and the lodge was where guests came to stay and relax after a hard day on the dunes. Plans had been drawn up for a golf complex, but they'd recently found out the project was compromised by a Site of Special Scientific Interest (SSSI), which in effect meant it was protected for future generations, making the prospect of getting permission to build anything on the site slim to zero.

Somehow, photographs from this site had managed to find their way into Trump's orbit. He knew what he saw, and he liked it straightaway. He told an executive to head over there and said, "Go get the land." A large chunk was bought from Tom, and then negotiations began with the neighbors—and DJT had bought most of the land in 2006 without ever seeing it in advance. He just knew he had to have it.

Now I could see why. It was astonishing.

Mr. Trump would later say, "God has done most of the hard work; all we need to do is add the greens and fairways." So, straight after that hearty breakfast, we had a tour of the property, the development team and me: planners, civil engineers, environmental consultants, cost consultants . . . the list went on and on.

Trump had wanted to submit the planning application yesterday, and he was very frustrated at how long things were taking; he felt the pace was way too slow, and it was tough to disagree with him. However, then the planning system in this part of the world was traditional—some would say archaic—and not the most welcoming to developers from the other side of the Atlantic. I needed to work out who everyone was and what they all did, and then I had to work out the issues in getting the application to submission. Trump was clear that he wanted the project in, approved, and work begun before the end of the year, and it was already March.

My predecessor in this role had already moved on, and Trump was telling me that we were months behind schedule. It was clear at this stage that I didn't understand the spectrum of issues: the legal, environmental, and even the practical problems with the neighbors, who were quite happy to develop their own houses and sites but didn't want anyone else doing the same. It had so many challenges. I was a novice, and I was already behind the eight ball. My boss was frustrated at the delays and wanted things moving right away, and I didn't know whether that was achievable with the team assembled by someone else.

The dinner the evening before had been all about pleasantries, but I knew I had to start the next meeting after breakfast by stating how disappointed I was with the team's performance so far. We were months behind schedule, and I was there to rectify that and get things back on track. I had to go backward to go forward and get this team moving. One of the group didn't think the time frame was achievable and walked away there and then. That was a bit of a shock, I can tell you. I'd never seen that kind of defeatist attitude before. Ever.

Talking about it is easy, but put yourself in my position: I was thirty-six or so at the time, no seasoned pro, they were experts in their field, in a different jurisdiction no less, and I didn't know the rules. It would have been tough enough in the United States, but I was in a foreign country. I fired a couple of consultants, but it set the tone for how things were going to be. I soon realized that the reason for the delay was that no one was driving the project. I went back and forth as often as I could—probably a couple of times a month— and talked to consultants, learning about all the issues, from things like what the planning laws were (as a lawyer I was naturally drawn to this) to what the challenges, time frames, and obstacles were, and just getting to know the rules. Then, of course, I had to delve into everything else, like the road, environmental, engineering, and drainage issues; the whole golf course design; and public consultation. Every day I was on site I was checking in with Trump and letting him know the details, whom we'd met and what was happening.

I remember standing on the dunes one day, with the sun setting way off in the distance to the west, and Trump saying to me over the phone, "You know what, George, you have the greatest job in the world. I'm jealous that I'm not there with you now just looking at that scenery."

You'd think building a golf course would be relatively easy, but the complexities of getting it off the drawing board and into the reality of execution are unbelievable. You can figure out fairly quickly whether people know what they are talking about, and I had to trim some more people and hire a few others. That was what we were used to doing in New York, but here it was an alien concept, and we had to change the whole mind-set from a slightly parochial, laid-back one to one with a sense of purpose, turbocharging it.

It's nerve-racking, to say the least, when environmental consultants and quasigovernmental organizations are still saying that a project will never get passed and you're pushing a team costing tens of thousands of dollars a month forward into the seeming dark. Those other developers had looked at the site and walked away. Trump stepped in where they had feared to tread—and, of course, he was subsequently proved to be right. In fact, time and time again, people would say he would never achieve what he had set out to do—and time and time again, he would prove them wrong.

Within thirty days I thought I'd righted the ship. I'd gotten rid of the weak links and had hired others, and I'd gotten everyone appreciating the sense of urgency that was coming from the top, from DJT. Not only did they understand it, but they agreed to my deadlines. That was my first challenge: taking an inefficient group of individuals and turning them into a team that pulled in the same direction and understood what they needed to do and respected and recognized the time constraints.

All along Mr. Trump was saying, "You'll figure it out and have a lot of fun with this." When I was back in New York and sitting in his office, we'd have these comprehensive meetings to discuss the course layout, design, facilities, and all the other minutiae that are needed to make this kind of project work. DJT knew every inch of that golf course and could see it clearly in his mind as we talked. He could remember the location of tee boxes and where they sat in relation to the dunes and even small hills and dips in the sand. He could picture every blade of grass.

There was no doubt in his mind, no suggestion that this wouldn't work; he was determined to get the complex and golf course he wanted, where others had said it just couldn't be done. We pushed hard and put in the planning application by June; it was a monster. It was a complex and massive undertaking. It wasn't perfect, but we got it in and responded to a round or two of the usual requests for additional information and dealt with the public consultations.

The first part of my education was complete, and I was now a pretty good expert on how to navigate the vagaries of the planning process. Despite smashing through numerous hurdles, the golf course was built and is now enjoyed by thousands of people every year and is considered one of the best in the world. There wasn't a day that went by when Trump wasn't pushing the envelope on every single decision, whether it was trying to get the most out of a contractor or trying to get a different perspective on a legal decision. He was about testing boundaries and exploring angles.

We always knew that the best parts of that golf course were where the SSSI was, and we were under pressure to move it inland, away from the North Sea. DJT didn't want to go there or even discuss it. He didn't want it routed away from the sea, and it became a constant battle even with our consultants. We spent so much time trying to get a result that they didn't believe was attainable. However, Trump wouldn't compromise the quality, and it was a daily struggle to push every member of the team toward a goal that some felt was unobtainable. The result we were looking for had never been accomplished in the history of UK planning. Other courses had been built and an SSSI accreditation given afterward, but it had never been done in advance. We have tremendous respect for the environment, but the area we were looking to develop composed less than 5 percent of the SSSI—and 95 percent of it remains untouched, despite what the fake news has written or said about it. There was an imperceptible environmental sacrifice, but the business benefits more than justified the change. In addition, the overwhelming majority of the neighbors supported what we were doing and continue to support the property.

It was standard practice for us to examine opportunities and prospects that others considered unachievable—that's what made us different and helped us stand out from the crowd. The world of real estate development requires vision, patience, and drive. The easy way to make your mark is to go and see a site and envisage it in the future. Some people will see a site with the potential for some development opportunities, but we always looked further, dreamed bigger, and imagined it better. We saw a hotel, a cluster of homes, and even a golf development where few others would have considered it possible. As the time of this writing, the organization is looking at the prospect of taking that vision even further with the next stage of development, modeled on the great estates of Scotland and driven by my great friend and executive vice president of the development Sarah Malone. Despite all the rancor and bitterness, DJT still sees Scotland as his spiritual homeland and something he values and treasures.

He pushed harder than ever before, driven by the constant reinforcement to look at things differently and aspire to greatness where others were too afraid or didn't have the means or desire to take the risk. Trump has made his career of conquering the unconquerable. Also, look at what he has achieved. When he later said he would run for president of the United States, people scoffed, laughed, and poked fun at him, but I knew he could do it. I knew he would do it—and look who's laughing now.

He did it with this incredible golf course, and he did it with the presidency—and the two were similar in the way that he refused to yield, refused to stop driving on, and refused to believe it was impossible despite the professional naysayers.

I will never forget being with him at Mar-a-Lago on Super Tuesday. I was with Eric; Corey Lewandowski, Trump's campaign manager; Keith Schiller, Trump's personal bodyguard; Dan Scavino, now the White House social media director; and Hope Hicks, who would serve as Trump's White House director of communications. Everyone was huddled around a big-screen TV in a room tucked out of the way at that magnificent club just watching the results flow in, and it was clear that Trump had a tremendous victory. There's no other way of describing it. Eventually everyone piled out of the room, and it was just him and me. He was preparing himself to go out to give his speech, knowing that the Republican nomination was in his grasp.

I could hear the noise of the hustle and bustle outside as maybe a thousand supporters congregated and waited for him to give that victory speech. I congratulated him and said, "You're one step forward toward becoming president."

He turned to me and very calmly answered, "We still have a long road to come, George. There's a long haul ahead." Then he walked on ahead toward the tumult. The noise got louder as we walked toward that famous ballroom, and as we entered, the place erupted. It was a fantastic place to be that night. He was confident, but he was ready for a fierce battle ahead—and that was what Scotland was, but no one does this better than him. If you're patient and in a protracted, litigious situation, you can't allow yourself to get overwhelmed; you have to go day by day and make one move at a time. You have to keep everything in perspective and win one little battle after another.

Even though it sounds so simple, many people can't do it. You have to be organized, diligent, and capable of taking one step after another, or it can all become an overwhelming mess, and you end up in the swamp. I learned that diligence, patience, and little advances—take a little ground, push another step, grab another inch, keep chipping away—are the routes to success. And that's what we did in Scotland.

This is a man who doesn't believe in the word "impossible." For Donald J. Trump everything is possible, and everything is within his grasp.

CHAPTER 7

The Donald J. Trump
I Know

The alarm blared, and I rolled over to switch it off. The blinking lights of the clock showed it was early—5:45 a.m.—but twenty-two stories up in the New York sky, it was the start of my morning. It was a typical day for me: roll out of bed in my corner apartment in Trump World Tower and pad across the floor to go switch the coffee on in the kitchen. There I could see the East River and some of my skyline neighbors also beginning to get going for the day ahead. As I wandered into the living area to flick my laptop on and catch the early-morning emails that were flying in from other parts of the world, I could see the Empire State Building and Chrysler Building and their beautiful spires in the sky. I never got tired of that view. Even before I genuinely managed to get myself into gear for the day ahead, and certainly not before my tie was on properly, I was checking in with colleagues and property managers wherever they happened to be and in whatever time zone their property was located. For many of them, they were well through the morning already.

Those calls done, I was ready to head into the office and prepare for a busy day, which was going to end with a planning board meeting in Westchester County for our project at Seven Springs. I hadn't been with the organization that long, maybe a year or so, but I was well into the swing of the operation and wanted to hit the ground running for the day to come.

Down the elevator, through the sleek lobby, and out into the dawn as the sun began to show its early rays and with it the prospect of a beautiful New York day looming. I was already focused on the emails and calls I'd given and received, and I almost missed my regular Dunkin' Donuts stop before I made it to Fifty-Seventh and Fifth and the office proper.

The twenty-sixth floor of Trump Tower has a beautiful, thick ivory carpet that sweeps throughout the space. My own office, about two hundred square feet, with its tremendous views of Fifth Avenue, was only a few short steps away from the boss's, and I started out by reviewing the day's press cuttings to see what they were saying about our properties and projects, because news reports and politicians' reactions to them could have a real impact on how those developments would progress.

I needed to look at the Seven Springs project for that night's planning board meeting, which Eric would drive us to, and then it was time to check in with the boss, with the first catch-up meeting of the day with all his execs.

He had been working in his apartment for hours before I'd even arrived. No one in the company ever worked longer hours than he did. He'd be up at the crack of dawn and work long into the night to get things done. He would often make and take calls from before six a.m. and would usually finish his day at some dinner, event, reception, or other business meeting within the Manhattan, or even the global, corporate world.

I wasn't sure how I would go about seeing him when I first joined the company. Should I schedule an appointment, should I call his secretary, how would I approach him? It turned out that he has the proverbial open-door policy, with few exceptions, and I always felt welcome in his office. I'd pop my head in the door, and if there was something he was busy with he would always politely tell me to come back in two minutes. I never felt intimidated, because despite his public persona, which many find overwhelming, he is extremely approachable, down-to-earth, courteous, and happy to hear what you have to say when you deal with him privately. I can't say that he always follows the advice put before him, but I can say unequivocally that he welcomes differing opinions and viewpoints. I was never apprehensive about speaking my mind, and I never hesitated to speak freely about my views on any given matter.

There would of course be the usual pleasantries and banter before we pressed on with the tasks of the day. I walked in with a list of issues that I intended to deal with that day, and I shared my thoughts with him, discussed strategy, and made sure that my agenda was in line with what he expected. It was a sensible, healthy chat, if a somewhat robust one at times, to ensure we were getting the best we could from whatever investment we were talking about at the moment. There was his L-shaped desk, up against the wall to the right, a large, traditional oak desk covered in newspapers, magazines, cuttings, documents, plans, and the ever-present glass of Diet Coke.

His office was an inspiring space dominating the East Side and looking out over the incredible vista that is Central Park. It was a long way away from the early days of working in an office in Sheepshead Bay, Brooklyn, with his father, Fred.

I remember one time when we had a couple of foreign government guys in the office who were desperate to get DJT to help them with a particular deal that was going down involving the Trump empire. We had gone through the usual negotiation, and it was clear that we weren't quite rolling over and helping them the way they expected us to. As the chat got more heated—although it remained utterly focused and polite—and we batted back and forth over the crux of the matter, Trump got an urgent call patched through, and the discussions came to a temporary halt. There was no question of our leaving the office; Trump never expected people to get out just because he was speaking to someone else. He never felt that was the right thing to do—it was courteous and sensible to get through the call and carry on with the meeting at hand. That's just the way he is.

The others visibly relaxed during this little break and looked around the comfortable office, as all people did whenever they were in there. The office was like a museum, full of memorabilia that chronicled Trump's deals, his battles, his victories, and his accomplishments, and that cataloged the people he'd met and dealt with from all walks of life. It was a fun place. He kept three chairs in front of his desk and a couch up against the window, but you couldn't sit on it, because it was full of footballs, boxing gloves, basketballs, hockey sticks—really cool stuff that had been given to him. The couch was almost like a sports hall of fame! We just chatted about the world and what was happening, and, inevitably, the conversation swung back to what was on display in this fantastic office that dominated the New York skyline. We chatted about some of the sports memorabilia that lay across the windowsill, and they asked why there were so many baseball bats in the office. I don't know where it popped into my head from, but I suppose there must have been a mean streak in me because I blurted out that they came in handy when we had a rough negotiation.

It was clearly a windup, and I expected howls of laughter, but they just kind of sat stock still and looked at each other, unable to work out what to say. It was clear they thought that I was serious and they were terrified that if things didn't go their way they might not get out of there with all their teeth in place!

It was crazy but utterly hilarious. And I didn't think it right to clarify the matter.

Well, hell, this was New York, after all.

One of the first questions I invariably get asked when I

meet people and they learn that I worked alongside him in one way or another over fifteen years is: Have I ever met him? It's a really intriguing and interesting question, because it speaks to the perception that Trump operates in this massive, global empire. Those asking it assume he spends all his time in a princely tower, surrounded by security guards and celebrities. They figure he makes only rare appearances before vanishing into the ether again.

It makes me laugh because in reality—and despite its massive global footprint and outward appearance of being a big conglomerate—the core of the organization is a small, very tightly knit group of no more than a few dozen executives and lawyers who often wear many hats and perform a variety of functions. I think that his son Don Jr. has put it best: "We're the world's largest mom-and-pop company." Together, they run a family business in which decisions are made very quickly by a small group of people—and, when he was still there, ultimately by DJT. On a practical level, he was involved in virtually everything, from making the final decisions, questioning budgets, and chasing results to asking for changes to be made to developments.

Throughout the day, I would periodically check in to let him know how a phone call had gone or to show him pictures of progress being made. My workday would end in the same place as it began: everyone would gather in his office and talk about the day's events and what was happening tomorrow. Some of these meetings could be challenging and tense, but on other occasions, they would be a lot of fun, with much laughter. We were a very tight team of trusted and respected executives who operated with Trump's blessing and support.

Sure, if we got things wrong we'd get our asses kicked, but we knew that he wanted us to succeed, and he gave us the freedom to get on with that job. You were never dismissed or told that he was too busy; he made time to speak with the people who were working on his projects. He always wanted to know what was going on.

This particular day I went in there and thought that I'd said something intelligent in an interview that had been printed in a newspaper. In about five seconds it became crystal clear to me that he disagreed and had wanted me to say the exact opposite. When it came to dealing with the press, he was almost always right in the long run. You win some and you lose some, but he would clarify the position that he wanted us to take going forward. I would take whatever actions as necessary to get that point across in future interviews. Do it differently and move on.

The view in DJT's office is breathtaking; there can't be many better views of Central Park elsewhere in the city. You can see the Plaza and the GM building—two buildings that at one point he owned, remember—and Central Park in the near distance. That view was an exciting reminder of the incredible projects he'd undertaken in the past. It was only in 1971 that Trump moved into Manhattan real estate. Who knows where he might have been if he hadn't decided to head into the city?

His father had achieved so much success in the outer boroughs, and many people would have stayed where they were and continued to operate in the area they knew so well: If something isn't broken, why fix it? He could have continued to develop outside Manhattan, and that's what conventional wisdom would have mandated: keep it going. However, that's not the Donald J. Trump way. He had the guts to move into Manhattan, where, frankly, you can either succeed or get buried. This is a fundamental characteristic of Trump. If I had to come up with a handful of words or phrases to describe him, they would be "insightful," "risk-taker," and "listens to his gut." However, that's not to say he takes unnecessary risks; rather, he takes mitigated risks backed up by amazing instincts.

That initial decision to go and build a high-rise on Fifth Avenue after his success acquiring the Commodore Hotel with the Hyatt group in 1976 and creating the Grand Hyatt was a bold move for someone who had done midlevel, midmarket condos in the boroughs—and it could have destroyed him. The Grand Hyatt, built in the struggling Grand Central area, ended in 1996 when the Hyatt corporation bought DJT's half share in the hotel for $142 million.

That was some deal. Anybody in real estate knows that when you put up a twenty-story building, it's hard, but when you go to forty-five floors and above, the risk level rises exponentially.

The situation on the twenty-sixth floor of Trump Tower is so very different now, of course. That central hub, the scene of so many battles and deals, laughter and fights, is now quiet and calm. The doors to the office are locked, and the memorabilia is boxed, cataloged, and piled up. Some of the framed magazine covers and the like are bedecked with Post-it notes decreeing whether they will go into storage or join many other pieces of fascinating insights into the mind of

Donald J. Trump when they hang on the walls of the presidential library one day.

It seems so strange to think that the images, photos, and cuttings, and the variety of gifts, awards, and other objects collected over several decades, will one day become the heart of what will essentially be a museum dedicated to this controversial man. It'll be odd for me to go there—and I will go there—one day and see all this stuff again, stuff that was so much a part of my day-to-day life.

However, this particular day, when ordinary workers were preparing for their journey home, we were wrapping up, ready for the two-hour drive to Westchester County, with Eric at the wheel, and the planning board meeting to come.

Life at Trump was never routine or mundane, that's for sure . . .

CHAPTER 8

Travels with My Blue-Collar Boss

Traveling on board Donald J. Trump's plane was like nothing I'd ever witnessed before. Even though I'd traveled extensively, it was almost always in coach, and I'd only ever enjoyed the glory of business class a handful of times. Before I worked for him, I'd only ever flown on a small private plane once, and even then, I had thought I didn't belong there, and the surroundings overawed me.

However, Trump didn't make you feel like that or that you shouldn't be there. He wanted you to be comfortable, although he's clearly proud of and enjoys what he has, as anyone would expect. He did simple things to make people feel relaxed and at home, like taking people on tours of the cockpit. I always enjoyed traveling on his plane, that amazingly opulent Boeing with his name emblazoned down the side. You certainly knew when he was coming!

It was always a fun environment. There was still work present, but it was a pretty lighthearted place to be, one in which we frequently watched movies and played cards and the like. We were always ripping on each other; you certainly had to have a good sense of humor to survive some of those plane journeys! If you couldn't take the banter, it could prove to be a long trip.

Even though it was amazingly grand and glamorous—a private 757 with huge bedrooms bedecked in gold and with mahogany conference tables and the like—it was a relaxing environment and not at all stuffy. Everyone respected that it was Trump's plane and what he'd achieved, but at the end of the day, he interacted with you in a way that made you feel relaxed and that you were welcome on board. There were always lots of great movies and food to sit down and enjoy as you traveled across continents. There's nothing like watching classics like *The Good, the Bad and the Ugly* on a widescreen, surround-sound TV at 35,000 feet.

In the early days of the construction of his Aberdeen project, before we rebuilt MacLeod House, Don Jr., DJT, and I would frequently stay in a small building that was formerly a horse stable and had been temporarily converted into office space with several bedrooms. Nice, but not exactly what you would call luxurious. I remember one time in 2008 when we left New York just before eight p.m. and traveled through the night, arriving in Aberdeen at about seven the next morning. As the doors opened and we climbed down the steps, the air felt cleaner and crisper than in New York, inevitably transporting me back to my childhood and summer holidays on the Isle of Lewis. Once we'd managed to negotiate the tiny airport and its archaic arrivals hall and customs facility, we were whisked across the few short miles to the development site and the office base and handful of rooms that we'd managed to convert ready for the development.

As we pulled up outside the old horse stables that now offered the first glimpse of Trump's empire in Scotland, the smell of freshly cooked bacon and eggs hit our nostrils. A wonderful local cook would come help keep the eggs and bacon flowing and the coffee bubbling whenever we were in town. We dumped our bags in our rooms—DJT and Don stayed in two of the rooms on one side of the stables, and Keith Schiller and I took the two rooms on the other side. Trump would have it no other way. He wanted to stay on site with his people, he wasn't fussy and didn't want anything more than anyone else, and he enjoyed doing it that way, just bunking down among the team amid the ongoing building work that was part of his vision.

We all sat down for breakfast together with fires crackling in the background and strategized about what was happening that day, whom we were going to meet, and what we needed to do. It was always busy, and there was always great banter. To me, that's the sign of a great team. It was so much like a family; it was the same dynamic. Not a group of guys who just worked together, but a tightly knit crew who looked out for each other. It just wasn't corporate at all.

We were lean and mean, and we could get decisions made quickly, and we trusted each other even when the boss wasn't there. In big corporations, decisions can be made by a committee, double-checked, analyzed, and audited, and so it's months down the line before anything gets done. We'd often have an idea over breakfast—the relocation of a green or bunker, or to drive a fairway left or right—and we'd decide it there and then. It was pretty unique and a stark contrast from both corporate America and what the perception of our organization was like. We were agile and could make things happen.

In the evening, everyone would relax together, having steaks and hamburgers, simple, plain but tasty food. We dined in the same restaurants as anyone else, and there was no special treatment, no private rooms, just Trump and the team in the restaurant with everyone else. People loved it, and we all loved it. Invariably, other diners who saw what was going on would come up to me and ask, "What's he doing here, and does he do this all the time?" And, yup, that's just what he did.

I remember him once having dinner with Alex Salmond, the former first minister of Scotland, who turned out to be an egotistical jerk-off. The first time he and Trump met was in New York for a Scottish government event. I kept getting these ridiculous calls from his office with concerns about where DJT would eat, and his dietary requirements and the like, and I kept trying to tell them that he would want some regular restaurant downtown and to eat with everyone else. He's just not into stuffy restaurants.

Instead, they chose a high-end French restaurant, and

there was not a word of English on the menu. It was so fussy, and I remember sitting there thinking, *Oh my God, what have they done here?* All Trump said after studying the menu was, "All I want is a shrimp cocktail and a steak." However, those stupid government officials wouldn't listen to me, or probably it was more likely that Salmond wanted to show off. Trump would later famously call him a "totally irrelevant has-been," and I'm sure this foolish outing didn't help with that impression.

Trump is happiest when he's just going out for normal meals like you and me. He's a hot dogs–and–Diet Coke guy, not a champagne-and-caviar guy at all. Again, Don Jr. used to say, "He's just a blue-collar guy with a large bank book."

His interaction with the teams meant he could hold court with anyone: bankers, lawyers, whoever. However, at the same time, when he came on a construction site, he knew precisely what was going on. He also spoke the same language as the tradesmen, and they were always impressed by his knowledge of the details. That's not always the case: I've worked with people who can look at floor plans in a boardroom but are lost once on site.

Trump, on the other hand, had intimate knowledge of the details of construction, whether it was a high-rise tower in an urban environment, a renovation of a country property, or, of course, when he was building a golf course. Without being pretentious, that attention to the fine detail was reflected in the end product being of the highest quality. The Trump Organization may not have the most, but it has the best.

He was very generous, taking us all to high-profile events, from a private box at the US Open, golf and tennis, to Roger

Waters, Broadway shows, and baseball games—for example, on the opening night of the new Citi Field ballpark and the first Mets game, I went along with him and Melania, and that indeed was a once-in-a-lifetime experience.

Melania, incidentally, is one of the most decent people I have ever met, and, like her husband, she immediately makes you feel welcome and appreciated. She's an incredibly elegant, gracious, and kind person, and I've had the pleasure of being on several trips with her and her parents, who are also such lovely people. I found her to be intelligent and warm, and I hate it when people denigrate her, because she doesn't have a bad word to say about anyone. She indeed is a rare, kind, and generous soul. She's so down-to-earth and approachable, as are her parents. They would often come to Scotland with us, and they were just a typical family—unaffected by the noise that surrounded them.

Yet Melania isn't a docile person in the background. She has her own views of the world, and anyone who spends any time with her knows that. It speaks volumes about her as a person, so kindhearted and with a caring way about her and a real sense of humility. When she first became first lady, I had to call her a few weeks after the election about a particular issue, and it was incredible to think of her occupying the White House. It was surreal, because she congratulated myself and Alan Garten, Trump's chief legal officer and EVP, on our new promotions—it was really funny, since we had called to praise her!

I went to the US Open at Winged Foot—by the way, my brother-in-law's family had been members there for generations, and when I went with DJT I got even better access and hospitality than they did—and to restaurant openings, and Trump invited me to play golf at his clubs in the New York area. I didn't feel an obligation to go to these things because it was my boss inviting me. I went because it wasn't work, it was fun, and I enjoyed his company. That's not something you can say about many bosses at all. In most organizations, if the boss invites you to an event, it's not relaxing, but that certainly wasn't the case with him; it was just great fun, and it had a long-term aim, as it also cultivated loyalty and helped you get through the tough times when they occurred.

I knew when he was happy and when he wasn't, so I always knew where I stood, and in a society where everyone is now so concerned with not offending someone or couching a message in a way that everyone is comfortable with, there's certainly something to be said for a straight-shooting management style. Trump wants his team to be straitlaced; there was no drinking or smoking in front of him, two habits that he despised. He expected the people who worked for him to be intelligent and out-of-the-box thinkers, honest and trustworthy. Trust is a big theme in The Trump Organization.

As approachable as the entire family is, they are who they are, and all those who worked for Trump would encounter information they would want to keep private, and everyone would and did honor that. Trust was a quality that was needed to ensure longevity in the organization—the family had to be able to trust you. That was necessary for many reasons, but at a simple level, there also had to be the discretion that Trump gave people, such as the power to make decisions and spend money.

We were expected to explain and account for every dollar.

Personally, I would keep running tallies of what was spent and where on every project I was working on, update them weekly, and let Trump know where we stood every few days. Unlike at publicly traded companies, where executives are beholden to amorphous shareholders, I would come to work every day and look in the eye the owner of the organization whose money I was spending. When you're trying to nail down what the company is like, that's a crucial point to keep in mind—it was his money that you were spending, and you needed to account for it.

Although they were good times—the golden era—another theme of his was that he didn't like to overspend, he didn't want to be ripped off, and he wanted to know he was getting the best deal. For me, being involved in real estate, we always made sure we got several bids; value for money was still a principle that was reinforced. When you work hard and take risks, you want to spend your money wisely.

Even when he was relaxing, he was working—it was what he loved to do. It blurred the line between work and fun, and a great example to illustrate that point was to play a round of golf with him. I enjoy golf, but although I spend a tremendous amount of time on the construction side of golf courses, I am by no means a scratch player. Trump approaches the game with enthusiasm and optimism. There's plenty of talk and banter; there's certainly a competitive element; and it all makes for a fabulous environment in which to talk about work matters. It's fast, it's ferocious, it's fun, but that arena can illuminate things differently. I've often found that taking work out of the office and into a more relaxing place can be an effective means of opening creative doors and stimulating different ways to tackle a problem or resolve an issue. Having fun out on the golf course and at the same time examining an issue can often lead people to a resolution that they might not have come up with in a formal office environment. So out on the golf course with Trump, there's always an element of work there. We would still be talking about issues, and as we were often playing our own courses, we would be talking about continuous improvement, like building new tee boxes, moving bunkers, and making the course better. As Andy Kjos, his superintendent at Trump International West Palm Beach, commented, "When he plays golf it's not like he is smoking cigars and then drinking cocktails with his friends by the pool afterward. He's working hard all the time."

Sometimes our best decisions were made outside the office during recreation time, and I've seen Trump take phone calls, meet with people on the course, and continue through all eighteen holes. Of course he's enjoying it, but he's more than capable of working and playing in equal measure.

CHAPTER 9

It's About the
Information, Stupid

On my first flight with Trump, there was myself and the legendary Keith Schiller, the former head of security for The Trump Organization, Trump's trusted bodyguard, and later director of operations for the Oval Office. Trump showed up a little later, and we were airborne within five minutes. It certainly beats United.

I noticed that two large boxes arrived on the 727 (which he later traded up to that magnificent 757) in addition to his suitcases. After takeoff, Keith went and got both of them, and they were filled with every type of magazine imaginable.

DJT sat there for the duration of the flight reading each one carefully, page by page, tearing out pages or articles that he found interesting or relevant. It was fascinating to watch.

While we certainly had our share of outstanding times on the plane, watching any one of an unlimited list of movies and live television and eating some of the most fabulous food you can imagine, it was also a great place to get work done. You're 35,000 feet up, free of distractions, among a small group of people, with the chairman of the company. We made much progress on various projects, prepared for hearings, and contemplated legal issues and so on while flying over the Atlantic.

Those pages that he tore out of those magazines would be distributed to individuals all over the world and throughout The Trump Organization. I got hand-written notes from my boss almost every day. He's quite a traditionalist at heart. He disseminated a lot of information and articles with handwritten notes. If he was reading something and it was relevant to the matter you were working on, or if he thought you would find it personally interesting, he would pass it along with a note. On any given day, I would get a load of handwritten notes from him, sometimes one or two words written on a Post-it, sometimes his incredibly neat handwriting across the top of a magazine article, letter, or email.

If you got a note from DJT, you knew it was from him because it was written in his trademark black Sharpie: bold, thick felt-tip, his letters all in caps with underlines for emphasis. There was always his trademark sharp "D" and the variety of peaks and troughs that are his unique signature. It certainly stood out, and there was no denying it was his moniker on the document. Whoever you were, from the head of state to an ordinary Joe, you got the same style of writing with the same thick, black felt-tip pen. It was sent to government officials, journalists, and everyone in between—Trump wasn't shy in sharing an opinion, his happiness, or his distaste.

This was part of what made the office environment different. There was a free flow of information in and out of his office, with the intent of keeping people informed, educating them, and often presenting a different perspective on an issue that we were working on.

One of the lessons I learned from him when I had just started at The Trump Organization—and as a person with virtually no press experience—concerned the power of the media and how important it was to manage them. My early experiences were tough and hard, but I learned how to play the game and realized that journalists were people like me who had jobs and deadlines, except that they were trading in the business of information. So I made it my priority, on Trump's recommendation, to get to know them on a personal level and never shied away from even the most difficult interviews, when I knew the organization was going to be maligned. Trump even told me how to stand correctly when being interviewed on TV so that I didn't look hunched and sinister. If you're going to get tips on how you look on TV, be sure to get them from the star of one of the biggest TV shows on the planet!

The philosophy he taught me was to spar with a hostile interviewer, and if the result was that a line or two was quoted offering my perspective, it was better than a "no comment" that provided nothing. In many instances, I often found that an objective, open-minded journalist could deliver the truth. However, there's nothing that makes me angrier than a journalist who acts holier than thou. It's become just another form of entertainment, and, unfortunately, it seems to be becoming the norm rather than the exception. Just check out your local newspaper hack's Twitter account, and I guarantee he is making spicy comments about what's going on in the world.

Many journalists also like to drag out and repeat spurious claims that have been made against Trump and treat them as fact when there's no credibility to the claims whatsoever, just because they've appeared in print before. It's such lazy journalism. I saw some of this during my own experience with a few of our projects that consumed years of my life. I knew every nuance, every detail, and every fact about those projects, and it was so frustrating to talk to a journalist who was asking questions from a position of absolute ignorance, misunderstanding, and misinformation, who couldn't even articulate the basis of the claims they asserted that they were exploring.

What was worse, either because of that lack of understanding, a lack of care, or just a desire to create an excellent narrative to boost their newspaper's sales, magazine circulation numbers, or TV viewing figures, journalists often went hunting for the so-called wounded party who opposed the project (usually without any validity) and gave them credibility where none should have existed. Most articles are too short for nuance and rest on a prepackaged narrative. The valiant David fighting against the billionaire Goliath is a prime example that kept getting rolled out.

Such journalists wanted only to be seen to be scoring a point against The Donald because it was easy and generated traffic. While I don't always agree with Trump's positions and methods, I'm happy that he is disrupting the status quo in terms of how our news is reported. It's about time. Politicians have never had an easier time talking directly to voters on social media, but then politicians have never been more afraid of making a gaffe either.

Either way, dealing with the media was a sport at The Trump Organization that we all enjoyed, and seeing the results of a combative interview were a routine part of the day. You win some, you lose some, but the effort was worth it. To this day, many of my harshest journalistic critics remain colleagues and some even friends. What most people don't realize is the complexity of the relationship between journalists and news-makers like Trump.

One reason people like me talk to the media is that it's really an exchange of information. At times, we are looking for information on a specific area the journalist knows about, which will be provided to us off the record in exchange for future access or the almighty exclusive.

Half the fun of covering Trump is the fight: What's he going to say, and what's he going to do? If he were a vanilla president, no one would be watching. We've had generations of vanilla presidents, and the 2016 vote proved the people were sick of it. They need each other: Trump needs the press, and the press need Trump; it's the perfect symbiotic relationship. In essence, it's the ageless clash between hero and villain that transcends culture and generation.

Then there's Twitter.

Following his election victory, my coauthor Damian Bates and I were sitting down having lunch with Trump in West Palm Beach with a couple of his golfing buddies. He went around the table and polled the group about Twitter. He prefaced the discussion with his declared love for Twitter but said that so many well-intentioned people had cautioned him to avoid or exercise some restraint with it because the tweets weren't helping him.

So everyone chimed in with his or her two cents. I acknowledged that I might not have been comfortable saying some of the things he did on Twitter, but his tweets and use of Twitter were a huge component of who he was. The formula worked, with the result being that he was only the forty-fourth person in history to become the president of the United States. In my opinion, Twitter was part of that chemistry; it worked, and I didn't think it would be smart to change the secret formula. We had a very similar discussion a couple of months later in the White House, and I said the same thing: "It works, so why change it?"

And he agreed. He said, "It's the modern form of communication; it's like owning a newspaper without the losses. I've got tens of millions of people that follow me on social media, and when I tweet the press immediately pick it up and broadcasts it and publishes it. In the past, you have to get filtered through the likes of the *Washington Post*, and now I can talk directly to people without that filter."

(For the record, he made the point to us at that lunch that he hated the term "tweet" because it sounds so juvenile. He prefers to refer to them as his messages on social media.)

This is a critical aspect of his personality. Many people

would say, "Every day I'm getting incoming and getting hit," and they would say, "I'm not going to tweet anymore," but this is a very different person—this is a man who knows what his customers, his base, wants, and he gives it to them. This could be detrimental to him, but he carries on because that's what his supporters want.

He acknowledged that Twitter gets him into trouble a lot, but he wants to communicate without any filter and be heard directly by the people who matter: voters and his supporters. That's the man he is.

CHAPTER 10

Let's Fight Back

I t's well documented that the Aberdeen project had its ups and downs, and one of the worst days of my career was seeing the initial proposal get rejected by the local government after working so hard.

The rejection took place at a hearing of councilors required to give us the outline planning permission that would allow us to press on with the basics of the project. It was fairly straightforward, and it was a hearing that we were supposed to have easily won. However, it turned into a lengthy and confrontational meeting. A lot was going on, and about halfway through, several motions were put on the table. As a lawyer, I didn't like what I was seeing, and I thought it wasn't going our way.

I stepped out of the room to call Trump and said to him, "I don't like the way this is going."

"Take hold of yourself and be calm," he replied, "and just go back in there and call me when you're done."

This was when he was trying to drive the company forward into new international spheres and was working day and night on getting *The Apprentice* out there. How he managed to stay so calm and measured amid all that noise, I'll never know. After a very contentious session, the vote on whether we should be allowed to proceed with the plans ended in a dead heat, a 7–7 tie. Under the Scottish procedural rules, the chairman of the committee can vote twice. So the chairman quietly confirmed it was a tie and added, "I get to vote again, motion defeated."

Just like that. The project had been strangled at birth.

It was one of those moments you see in movies: everything slowed down and went deathly quiet. I heard nothing for quite some time, as everything else went out of focus. Then I noticed that I was surrounded by everyone wanting to know what was happening and what would come next. I was trying to speak to our planning agents, and I couldn't even begin to think about what we were going to do. Inevitably, there was an absolute melee and a myriad of reactions. Some of our biggest detractors and opponents came up to laugh in our faces. Some people were angry we'd taken our development plan that far; others were angry that we'd lost and the project was in jeopardy—and through all this I had thirty different microphones thrust in my face.

While I had little sense of what we might do next, I was incandescent with rage. How could such a small number of councilors turn down such a significant investment in a part of the world that was crying out for diversification away from an oil and gas sector that was to face substantial challenges in the years ahead? In a daze, all I could say was, "If you want to do big business, don't do it in the northeast of Scotland." It was kind of awkward but all I could muster at the time. It hit the mark, and to this day, Scottish politicians talk about Scotland being "open for business."

My mind was racing: *What am I going to tell the boss? What the hell happens now?* I just wanted to get out of there. As I left the building, a BBC journalist jumped in front of me and said, "Has Mr. Trump heard about this yet?"

Well, no, he hadn't. I sat in my car and had to phone him and explain it to him—twice—because he didn't understand how a committee could have a tie, with the chairman, a self-confessed green campaigner who rode a bicycle to get anywhere, left to make the final decision. With the car surrounded, the team knew we had to get out of there to have some peace, to regroup, to consider our next moves, and, most important, to speak to Trump properly.

There were clearly some choice words, a lot of heat was rushing back and forth across the Atlantic Ocean, and, inevitably, we were all disgusted but more determined to get things done. It was a significant defeat for me on many levels, and I was crushed and furious. My emotions lurched all over, and I wasn't in a good place. However—you know what? While I initially took a beating from New York, later on that night, after enduring a global media onslaught in which every journalist piled on my back, I got a straight-forward call from Trump. It was about midnight UK time, and everything I had worked for had been dashed. He called me up, calmly asked me how I was doing, and quietly projected a message that has stuck with me: "Don't worry about it, get up tomorrow, regroup, and let's fight back."

It was clear that things had to change and we would have to take a different tack, so we fired a few people, but we knew we had to press on. Remember the pressure DJT would have been under at that time, with his crazy TV filming schedules and the empire rapidly expanding all over the place, but he cut through the crap and just calmly told us to have another go.

That was comforting on so many levels: I was re-empowered to pick up the sword and the shield and do what we needed to do. I woke up the next morning feeling like a new man, and despite the defeat, I was invigorated, and we fought like hell for the next year to finally get the job approved. There were many further ups and downs along the way, but after an enormous struggle, we got the project done.

On that night of the initial defeat, Trump was very measured; he gave me criticism, vented, and then backed me up, empowered me, and moved on. This wasn't unique to me, The Trump Organization, or the development—these are the lessons in life everyone has to face. And, man, did I learn a great lesson that day: it's how you process failure and how you regroup that is the measure of a man.

We have to guide our future generations and make them understand that failure is a part of life and learning how to get through it is more important than celebrating success.

People need to learn from their mistakes and failures and convert them to success.

Trump himself isn't averse to making mistakes. He goes with his gut, his instinct, on so many occasions and drives forward with the utmost confidence. He has no fear of making a misstep; he knows that he can quickly go back and correct a situation so that he can continue forward. DJT knows better than anyone that he isn't perfect, that inevitably he's going to make a mistake in public. It's about how you react to that that matters. As DJT himself says, "It's better to go seek forgiveness than ask for permission."

A senior member of a development team who had been a reliable and trusted performer for years decided that it was time to move on. He was a tough cookie, but the pace had taken its toll on him, and he wanted a less pressurized environment after years of backbreaking work at all times of the day and night. We were all upset, and while anyone is replaceable, there are certain people who, when you lose them, you feel it. I went into Trump's office to give him the news. He was surprised and upset and said, "I was just too hard on him." There was genuine sadness and regret that the guy was leaving us. Trump wanted to make sure the departure was amicable because he'd been a good guy, and he offered to write recommendations.

Even Donald J. Trump gets it wrong sometimes.

CHAPTER 11

I Never Read the Contract:
Buyer's Remorse

It was destined to be another long day, and the wind was already howling across the courtyard. I was a long way from home, working on another international project, and the chill was beginning to bite. It may have been only the early days of fall, but the first cold winds were sweeping in, and there was a light rain in the air—it was clear that the temperature was changing, and fast.

There was so much going on, so much to discuss and digest, but for some reason, I happened to glance at my Black-Berry. (Well, this was the best technology that 2008 could muster.) What I saw didn't make for pretty reading. The winds of change weren't just happening here on site; they were hitting the rest of the world, too.

I remember drawing a sharp intake of breath as I sought to comprehend what the hell was happening. The financial markets were in free fall. The Dow Jones plunged more than 700 points in intraday trading alone. And it seemed Congress had rejected a bill to try to rescue a banking system that was about to keel over and plunge the world into the most significant depression seen since the 1920s.

I tried not to panic; after all, I'd seen something similar before, but not quite as dramatic—or, as it turned out, as severe as this was going to prove. The last time we'd faced such warnings of financial doom was back in 1987 (oddly, within a few weeks of the date of the 2008 crash), when I was just a college sophomore, and we were all sent reeling by the 25 percent drop in the markets caused by Black Monday.

Standing in that courtyard, preparing for a string of further complicated and intense planning meetings that were to come that day, I tried to stay calm and rationalize the fact that markets plunge and inevitably—even if it takes an incredible amount of time—they rebound.

I managed to make a swift and garbled call to my broker at Goldman Sachs to reassure me that my investments were safe and that we should stay firm and let the market ride the waves. He seemed calm and measured, and there was little I could do other than take his advice and press on with the day's business. That's not to say I didn't feel worried and concerned that everything I'd built in the years up to that moment was very vulnerable. Even Goldman Sachs would eventually need support from the US government to ensure it didn't go the way of some of its corporate contemporaries: down the pan.

As of this writing—more than ten years on—we're still feeling the aftereffects and seeking confidence in our financial institutions. Some say it may well happen again—and not too far in the future.

Despite the nervousness that surrounded the tumultuous crash that was dragging down global financial institutions, there was no real sense of panic among the team at The Trump Organization. It's quite incredible to think how calm we were, given the potential for us individually, and the organization specifically, to face fiscal ruin. We were all seasoned enough to realize, though, that no matter how big the waves, how deep the losses, and how intense the hyperbole of the media, the crash had to come to an end sometime, somehow. We all sat around the table and discussed the craziness of what was going on for a while, but we inevitably got back to the issues of the day and cracked on with the project at hand.

Of course, we all know what happened next. Financial institutions that had spread loans around like confetti found that they had no liquidity left. The great con that was the subprime mortgage debacle turned out to be what everyone had always thought it was: lousy debt that wasn't worth the paper it was written on. As a consequence, some of the best-known names on Main Street, USA, suddenly vanished overnight despite having phenomenal reputations and incredible histories. Bear Stearns, Lehman Brothers, Merrill Lynch, Fannie Mae, and Freddie Mac all either collapsed or had to be rescued from the fierce flames of a roaring financial fire.

For The Trump Organization, the crisis wasn't the im-
pending doom that many people might have suspected or expected. As the first signs of the financial trouble that led to
the subsequent devastating crash began to emerge, DJT had
started to steer us in a new direction. The subprime mortgage debacle had seen money thrown about and real estate
beginning to overheat substantially, with prices rocketing
way beyond where they really ought to have been. As Alan
Garten, EVP and chief legal officer for the organization, saw,
several interrelated decisions helped direct the company away
from what could have been if not a shipwreck, then certainly
tricky waters to navigate. "Just before the crash happened,
if you went to Dubai or Panama—where I visited—the skyline was littered with cranes and development was going full
throttle," Alan said. "But the first hints of the subsequent
crash were beginning to show. Subprime mortgages were
being traded despite everyone knowing they were junk. . . .
Banks were offering mortgages at crazy levels without worry-
ing where the repayments were going to come from."

Trump's radar was clearly attuned to rising prices that had
the potential to hit the business. One thing Mr. Trump won't
do is overpay—whether that's for property or any other deal
that he's working on. He saw that land and property were
beginning to get too expensive and that there just weren't
any reasonable deals to be done, and so he started to back off
projects that others were still diving into in the vain hope that
they could still make a few bucks.

It also helped, of course, that his business could tilt toward
new opportunities and deals. Luckily, too, we'd sold out some

big high-rise condominium projects and did well—making a lot of money out of them.

Don Jr., Ivanka, and Eric were now fully on board, and they were beginning the significant diversification of the business. *The Apprentice* brought attention like never before and opened the door to licensing deals and opportunities that had never even crossed our minds, let alone our desks. It was a time of structural change in our business, and the timing couldn't have been better or more apposite. There was a lot of interest in low-risk areas, where we lent our name, expertise, and management abilities in exchange for very lucrative fees. These areas were broad and encompassed real estate, clothing, food and drink, and a myriad of other worlds.

As Alan remembered: "DJT was thinking, 'Why would I borrow half a billion dollars when I can basically become a Ritz-Carlton, Starwood, or Four Seasons? I can create luxury and reap the rewards and not have to invest millions with the subsequent risks.'"

Remember, this is a guy who said, "Why should I spend tens of millions of dollars on building a ninety-story building when I can get the same return—and more—by doing one season of *The Apprentice*?"

"He had the foresight to put a hold on future development because he saw that the market was beginning to overheat," Alan said about the beginnings of the financial crash, as he paced the floor of his Trump Tower office. "He knew that his money was better used elsewhere."

Tell me who else in the world wouldn't take that same

view? Less risk, less capital outlay, and better return on the investment? *Yes, please.*

All of us in the organization were seeing other real estate markets and developments getting killed as the crisis deepened. Projects were being interrupted midconstruction because the financial world had collapsed, and some residential projects were left in limbo as purchasers couldn't close on their apartments. We'd moved away from many of these kinds of projects, although not from all of them, and as the markets crashed it also became an incredible opportunity for us. We had cash—from licensing, from *The Apprentice*, from the great projects in New York, Las Vegas, and Chicago—and so we could pick up some incredible bargains; we got some real marquee properties for ten cents on the dollar, literally.

Were we lucky and in the right place at the right time? Absolutely, but we had done the things that put us in the right position to be lucky: we were diversifying, finishing lots of projects, had cash in hand, and made a lot of good-value deals among the chaos.

Also, we weren't the only guys out there picking up great deals, either. Distressed debt meant portfolios were being snapped up. Anyone with cash and bravery could pick up big-value deals for pennies on the dollar. Lots of people made good money. We've taken much criticism for some of these deals, but it was what many people were doing.

There was a lot of excitement as we filmed a couple of seasons of *The Apprentice* in one go, and the place was buzzing—it was indeed the golden era. Because of the market situation, some excellent properties that we'd never imagined we could get hold of were suddenly easily within reach. There were a lot of hotel and golf deals, and I was involved in many of them.

When others were contracting, we went through a rapid expansion. If you look at our golf portfolio, we had two or three properties when I started, and as of this writing, we have nineteen or twenty.

There was a real energy about The Trump Organization, and we were lucky to be there—some of my friends were at development firms that were dying, and it wasn't much fun when they could see us thriving. On one occasion, in true DJT style, I remember being in his office chatting, and he said there were a couple of banks that had gone under, and their guys had been so conceited and patronizing over lending money to us for projects—the sort of assholes who wanted to look big by making Trump squirm. Later that week, I saw a letter to the former CEO of one of these banks that said the same thing: "You arrogant SOBs, look at you now."

It was an era for us to utilize the age-old advice about the stock market: buy low and sell high. One of the classic bits of Trump philosophy over the years was "a perfect deal is made when you buy it." He knew that if you buy something for a relatively low price, then you're not going to lose. If you can get value at inception, it cuts out a lot of risk and makes things a lot easier. We were out there and doing it. We'd buy places, put our people in charge, do the renovations and improvements, and end up with an asset that was worth a lot more than we paid for it.

The Trump Organization wasn't entirely immune to the horrendous crash that quickly spread around the world and almost saw capitalism itself implode. Whole nations stood on the brink of bankruptcy. Alan remembered it well: "The first time I knew there was going to be a problem was when a European bank that had given a loan commitment to do a project in North America that we were involved in suddenly, around February 2008, faced a real problem. The developer was the same developer who built a very successful project for us that we sold out and presently manage.

"They had a hole in the ground, and the bank had a loan commitment, and it started to fail. The government of that European country stepped in to give it over $5 billion to bail it out, and it had to cut jobs.

"That was the beginning of the end," Alan said matter-of-factly.

The banks began to crumble, and a domino effect spread throughout the world's financial institutions—and the real estate market tumbled, too. "Everything was in the toilet. . . . All the cranes in Dubai and Panama stopped, people were abandoning cars at the airport to get home."

Trump was in the midst of building hotel-condominium projects in New York, Chicago, and Las Vegas, and the reverberations of the financial crisis put these projects in real jeopardy as partners struggled to come up with the funds to make sure they were completed at all, let alone on time.

However, DJT would have none of it. He believed in the buildings that he was developing, and their locations, and he wouldn't let them crash and burn—he insisted they would be finished and to the standards he expected. Inevitably, though, as the world reeled from arguably the most significant recession since the Wall Street crash almost eight decades earlier, he had to restructure the debt, and some elements of the projects had to change.

Alan remembered how people who had been clambering to sign up for these projects suddenly started to waver. "People who had jumped in as soon as they could with their deposits started to get nervous and realized that the good times of easy cash might well have gone. Where were they going to raise the balance for the condos they had bought?" Outstanding balances were due for the remaining 80 percent of the cost price of the apartments that they had put hefty deposits on, and there was no way they were going to be able to raise that kind of easy cash now.

There were people buying condos in hastily cobbled together investment clubs formed with friends and family members, each brought in on the promise of a healthy return, done quickly and with minimum risk. However, borrowing stopped overnight and the expected prices for condos and apartments were crashing, with some investors realizing their property was not worth anywhere near as much as the cost price. They screamed and whined and did everything in the book to try to get out of their commitments, despite their legally binding contracts and the fact they had entered the deal fully aware of the potential consequences.

"Some of the people buying into Trump projects were Realtors and speculators who thought they could get in quick, flip it, and get out fast with a healthy profit and little investment," Alan recalled. "But this began the busiest time of my career, as people desperately tried to find ways to escape their commitments and payments—they started claiming breach of contract or that they had been misinformed and so sued."

Some buyers knew there was nothing to be done but to walk away and wave goodbye to the deposits of several hundred thousand dollars—better that than continue with the purchase and be left with debts several times higher than their initial investment. Many others bit their lips and carried on, seeing their investment as a long-term pitch that they would eventually regain once the markets stabilized. Others did what Americans do best: they sued.

"We had a big trial in Chicago with a buyer suing to get their money back," Alan remembered. "After Trump testified, the jury ruled in our favor and awarded us our costs. The jury said it was 'buyer's remorse': you bought it, it's not what you thought it was and not worth it, and you want to walk away—well, that's buyer's remorse.

"It's like buying Apple stock when it's going up, and then it collapses, and you try to get out of it by saying you didn't think it could fail or you weren't aware that Apple got someone in China to assemble its iPhones."

Trump faced the same accusations: that he was the developer, but the contracts and information made it clear that he was partnering with others to provide the real estate.

"Most buyers settled, except one in Fort Lauderdale. Even then, the jury sided with us and said it was baseless, as the contract clearly stated that Trump was licensing his name to the development and even had clauses that if he didn't like the quality of the work he could pull his name off it."

Alan shook his head when he remembered that even in the developments that didn't go ahead, investors were suing for compensation on top of the deposits that were returned to them because the crash meant many of these projects were now no longer feasible. "At trial, we cross-examined one of the buyers in Fort Lauderdale, and he said: 'I never read the contract. I felt it was Trump and so I should never need to read it.' The jury found in our favor because they knew the contract was straightforward and watertight.

"In another case, one of the plaintiffs was a multimillionaire. At trial, he claimed that his signature was forged. People were trying to come up with any reason to get out of their responsibilities and debts and try to get some compensation from us."

Also, there were incredibly spurious reasons for some to take issue with the contracts, the deals, and even the cases themselves. "In one case, the plaintiffs claimed the judge was biased because the judge gave Trump his glasses to read a contract during the hearing!" Alan recalled.

These weren't easy times for Alan and his colleagues. "The animosity between the lawyers was like you wouldn't believe. I remember sitting in a restaurant in Chicago and getting a call to say the jury was coming back in and we had a verdict. I hopped into a cab and went past the ABC studio and saw the ticker tape saying, 'Jury Returns Verdict in Trump Case,' and I was thinking, 'Holy shit, this is it.'

"It was exciting stuff and was clearly decisive."

For Alan, the conclusion was pretty clear. "Reasonable people would see that we were in the right. Just because it was Trump, people would jump at us and see if they could get any money out of us. They all failed."

Throughout the years I've seen this so many times: people using the Trump name to promote their own agendas or gain attention for their businesses. I've seen cases in which objectors have no rational grounds to support their claims. They make arguments, cause a fuss, go to the media, and because it's Trump, they get the attention they want. It's nothing more than showboating, and it still goes on to this day.

However, this period in The Trump Organization's history was a great time. There was no panic, just opportunities and lots of hard work. For DJT, that's the art of the deal—and then he loves and nurtures those bargains he's made, rarely selling them off. He feels that if you buy good assets at a reasonable price they're worth holding on to for a rainy day.

And we haven't had too many rainy days.

CHAPTER 12

Searching for the Stars

In 2012, we were working on one complex project, and we were having extreme difficulty with our contractors. We were searching for an appropriate foreman to get in there and straighten things out. The interview process was frustrating, and we met so many candidates who didn't have the background, fortitude, or understanding to work with us and get the job done. When we finally did find the perfect match, we learned that he worked for a contractor that we were already very close with.

Once again, DJT made the call himself, explaining the situation to the company's owner and describing what we needed, stating that we'd found the perfect candidate—in his company—and seeking permission before we extended the offer to the guy.

In this instance, our friend was very candid that he needed this person to finish another job and asked that we wait. Trump had no problem with that response, and we ended up hiring someone else. How many other people—whether global executives or not—would accept that and back off?

In my interpretation, such actions are a sign of humility and exemplify the great deference Trump shows to preserving relationships and keeping his friends no matter how big or small they are. Much has been written and said about his ruthless pursuit of what he wants, but in reality, at heart, he is a man who wants to do the right thing.

Then there was my great friend and counterpart in Scotland Sarah Malone, the executive vice president of Trump International Golf Links Scotland. Here was a woman who, by her own admission, knew absolutely nothing about golf. She was an artist and a curator by training and was working as a curator-director of a military museum not far from our project in the north of Scotland when we hired her. Trump was looking for the perfect candidate to deal with the project on the ground locally and bring it to fruition. He spotted a newspaper article about her work at the museum and asked me to call her and meet up on my next trip over there.

I was bemused. However, I did as I was asked.

I met Sarah at a local hotel in 2008 where I was camped out while the project was in its infancy. I was watching a news bulletin about one of our projects with one of our environmental consultants, Ed Russo, and in came Sarah. I sat and spoke to her for about forty-five minutes, and my first impressions were that she was a brilliant, articulate, well-put-together individual. She had grown up in the area, was well connected and sharp as a tack, she knew the environment, and I felt we could trust her. I liked and respected her, but the director of a military museum was not necessarily what we were looking for. Real estate is a hard-hitting and demanding rough world, and I just wasn't sure she had the experience to assume that role.

I spoke with her many times over the course of the year and arranged for her to come to New York to meet Trump. He spent an hour talking to her and hired her on the spot.

So, what was it that he saw in her that I didn't? When we spoke about it afterward, I raised my concerns, and he said, "Look, she's smart, she'll represent us well, and I think she'll be trustworthy. She can learn the rest along the way. She'll get this job done and help create a fantastic product in her hometown that she and everyone else will be incredibly proud of."

When Trump asked her if she knew anything about golf, and she responded no, he said, "That's even better. I don't want someone on this project wasting their time playing golf!"

That was somewhat similar to when I'd had the conversation with him about Scotland, and I said I didn't know anything about golf. The hiring of Sarah—whom he often dubbed the Queen of Scotland—was a classic example of how when evaluating a person for a role, you don't need to focus on a specific experience or get a subject specialist, because it's all about the character and potential. A skill set is transferable, and traits like intelligence, trustworthiness, responsibility, and the ability to get things done are more important than a previous career path.

Trump spotted that straightaway with Sarah. She went on to achieve incredible things in Aberdeen. She is the brains behind an incredible development that will see new hotel accommodation, leisure facilities, sports complexes, and homes built on the site—with another golf course to boot, to make it a truly iconic and incredible golf facility that will be difficult to match anywhere else in the world. All that from a local woman who had no interest in golf and was working in a military museum.

Let's be honest: most jobs can be learned along the way if the person you have at the helm has the right character, attitude, and intelligence. In actuality, hiring anyone is a leap of faith at best; you'll never know what you've gotten until six to twelve months have passed. I've hired some people who appeared to be great and ended up being disasters, and I've employed others whom I had initial reservations about who ended up being stars. Trump taught me to look for a person's essential qualities, and you can see that he brings this same management style to bear in the White House.

It's not all about the seasoned pro—which, admittedly, is also sometimes needed—as Trump has shown. He's not plucked people from the same pool of political animals who keep turning up over and over again; he's tried to bring in fresh blood, with new ideas and enthusiasm. Sure, sometimes it doesn't pay off, but on many occasions, it's been tremendously successful. Aim for talent, keep an open mind, and you can achieve great things.

Things were tough for Sarah in the beginning, and I certainly didn't help make it easier for her. We pulled no punches in New York to see if she could stand it in the ring, but after working alongside her for ten years I know she is one of the most competent executives not only in the organization but across any company in the sector. I defy you to find anyone else with the same amount of knowledge about the intricacies of golf course and real estate development and operation.

Trump has been accused by many in the past for not promoting the interests of women. However, the truth is the opposite: he empowers them. And Sarah is a prime example of this. She became one of the most senior executives in the organization, and while there are others, no one is quite like Sarah Malone. As she said to me, "It was a shock to the system at first, and in the beginning, I didn't know what I'd let myself in for, but the chemistry was right, and I wholeheartedly believed in the vision and was prepared to fight for it." Sarah is tenacious and turned out to be a hardened warrior, and she ultimately won the battle for us.

Many people and organizations claim to be experts in the recruiting game, from headhunters who rely on specific methodologies and analytics to those fly-by-night operators who claim to know "exactly what you need." Trump relies on his ability to read people, and he has an unbelievable knack for taking people out of one arena and placing them in another, often without experience, because they are just the right person for the job. Experience and knowledge can come with time, but the right person is like a piece of a puzzle: it either fits or it doesn't.

The Trump Organization's senior vice president for design and construction, Mike Vergara, began his career with us as a chef, cooking personally for Trump and Melania. Now he leads one of the most critical and challenging sectors in the business—although to be fair, he did have a background in construction, as well as being a great chef!

Trump spots talent and nurtures it and sees opportunities for people where others may not. He's still doing it to this day in Washington.

Many times in life people fall into a rut. They're not happy with their decisions, they're not satisfied with their career, they're not happy with their lifestyles, and they fear that they're unable to make a change; they're trapped in a hole. The lesson here is that all of us have personality traits, personal characteristics, and various other skills that are transferable. It's a matter of having an open mind. Trump has relocated, replaced, and changed people who were okay with doing one thing and put them in another area where they then began to thrive.

Sometimes you have to have the confidence and comfort with yourself to take the proverbial leap of faith and look for something that you may love. Getting out of your comfort zone often leads to an opportunity that you could never have imagined.

Trump is an example himself.

How many times did you hear the press, the TV commentators, and the politicians dismiss his candidacy as a joke? How many times did you hear Democrats ridicule him, cheer him on in the primaries, and underestimate the challenge they faced? How many times did you hear even conservative experts say he had no chance of winning the most significant political role on the planet?

Just because something hasn't happened before doesn't mean it's impossible.

CHAPTER 13

Facing the Baying Mob

D JT once had to travel to Scotland to give evidence at a parliamentary hearing into coastal wind farm installations and their potential adverse impact on tourism. It was grand theater, of course, and the world's media was in attendance.

It was quite a peculiar experience to be in the building that is home to the Scottish Parliament—google it and you'll see what I mean. It looks like the builders kept abandoning one design for another as they went. It's especially stark sitting right next door to the classic beauty of the queen's official residence in Scotland: the Palace of Holyroodhouse. It was also ten times over budget when it was completed, which shows what kind of grasp on reality some of the politicians in that country have. They, of course, wanted their moment in the sun and tried to play DJT and make him look stupid, but he's not naive about these things and pressed on with his case.

As it all came to a climax, DJT wanted to go and speak to some people who had put themselves in the firing line by supporting his case. Mr. Trump wanted to thank these supporters personally, and as they were outside, he had to make his mind up about leaving or staying inside to ensure his safety. As well as the supporters, there was a whole gaggle of protesters, anti-Trump campaigners, and every manner of hooligan you can imagine outside. The police warned him that it wasn't safe for him to head out into the crowd and that he could be putting himself in real danger. Keith was imploring him not to go out and warning him that it could escalate very quickly and his safety was truly in jeopardy. However, this is a man who doesn't go back on his word, and he was determined to say thank you in person.

The scrum as he wandered out was utterly ridiculous. There were people everywhere, some mocking him, others wanting to say thank you for fighting the turbines, and other bystanders wishing to see what the fuss was all about. There was a handful of police officers, and Keith desperately tried to keep the rabble who wanted to get their hands on him at bay. Trump managed to say a few words to thank his supporters for their help protesting the protestors, and he was whisked away into the car that waited for him.

It was so out of control and very risky. This wasn't a bunch of librarians waving placards behind a rope. I don't think anyone would have blamed him if he'd ducked out the side, to avoid any potential personal risk and confrontation. The police were genuinely concerned. However, that's the way he is. The fact that he places himself at ordinary tables when he's dining in restaurants, and not in private rooms, or that he goes and joins the other members in the grill room at his golf clubs and doesn't like people fussing around him, says it all.

When Damian and I had dinner with him in the White House, there was no special treatment, no special menu. He ate what we ate. While it was amazing to be dining in the White House and the food was incredible, it was like just having a bite to eat with a friend. As often as not, he's likely to show up at the Old Post Office—now known as Trump International Hotel Washington, DC—for dinner, because he wants to be where other people are and see what's happening away from the protective ropes.

Leaving behind the pomp and ceremony and just heading out and talking to ordinary people has stood him in good stead when it comes to diplomacy. He doesn't need the teams of diplomats to set up premeetings before meetings are held about meetings of meetings. This is a guy who wants to sit across the table from his contemporaries, talk, and thrash some things out. He wants to get things done.

That ability to engage with people, from the doorman on the street of a condo block to the president of a global superpower, shows his ability to participate at every level and to get things done. He's just as comfortable in rarefied atmospheres as he is when he's eating meatloaf at his desk.

Moreover, he never forgets his roots or his friends.

CHAPTER 14

Listen and Learn

Whenever you turn on the TV these days, you hear lots of critics making claims that DJT doesn't listen—particularly to his advisers, but generally to his staff, the people, or anyone at all, for that matter. There's a perception that he sits in this glorious gilded bubble, whether that be in the White House or Trump Tower, and he dictates his decisions without any input from, or conversation with, anyone else.

Thinking the experts are wrong is not the same as thinking everyone is wrong. This is a crucial distinction.

In my many years of working with Trump, I've found that he listens to people more than anyone else I've ever worked alongside. That doesn't necessarily mean he takes orders or ends up agreeing with everyone! He has strong views on many issues in a vast array of areas. However, there's always a process, and chances are, before he makes a choice, he's discussed the issue at hand with many people from many different backgrounds.

DJT would be the first to admit that he doesn't have all the answers, but he knows how to get them. He knows that lurking within every one of us is an opinion on good practice, style, or what is considered right or wrong in any particular context. For example, when The Trump Organization is designing a structure such as the facade of a clubhouse, it will hire several different architects to come up with independent renderings for the site. The renderings would sit on Trump's desk for several weeks, and anyone coming in and out would be asked, "Do you prefer A, B, or C?"

Trump was always absolutely fascinated by their answers and their rationale for coming to a given conclusion. In the days after receiving input from dozens of people, some of whom would have been entirely unrelated to the organization, the end product could well have been a combination of all three or something altogether new. The secretary coming in with his can of Diet Coke would have been asked what she thought of the designs as much as a visiting head of state or a leading company director. It didn't matter what your position, Trump was interested in your view and why.

The bottom line is that we ended up with a decision that was commented on and therefore improved, and we had the perfect design for what we were looking to accomplish. The same could be said with the fixtures, furnishings, rugs, lighting, and everything else that was required to complete the job. It was often hilarious to see some of the biggest names on the planet—from rock stars to basketball heroes—being asked what they thought of a particular carpet sample or design for a clubhouse when they were in for a chat with the boss. I understand his thought process, though. Thinking back to a conversation that I had with him while walking the site in Aberdeen, I recall he said to me that people would often ask him how he succeeded, and he told me that the answer is quite simple.

We were walking across the top of the dunes—which he subsequently renamed the Great Dunes of Scotland—and we were chatting about his thought processes and how to make sure that the final product was exactly right for the location it was in. It was a glorious day with very little wind, and the sun was shining down on us in this beautiful part of Scotland—me, Keith, and him. The conversation came around to how one should make sure the end product suits the marketplace, and to that question he always gets asked about why he's been successful. As we looked out over the calm North Sea, he said, "It's quite simple. I know what people want, and I give it to them."

That was that.

Experts are great, but the experts aren't usually the ones who have to live with the outcomes. The golfer plays the course. The soldier fights the war. The taxpayer pays the bills. DJT knows what people want because he asks them. It's a simple and effective strategy that has served him well. His approach is straightforward: continuously ask people—from every stratum of society—questions about what is it they like and would want to see in a hotel, golf club, or apartment. So it continues to this day.

Whenever I've met with DJT, he's asked my opinion in conversations about a whole myriad of issues and current world events. There's nothing wrong with that. He likes to know what other people think and where they are coming from. Getting a difference of opinion can ultimately lead to a solution that you would never have contemplated if you didn't explore every option. Trump would often radically change the design of a building based on the reaction of others.

I remember once when we were working on an international development that was just massive in scale, and the renderings looked like they had come out of Narnia or some scene from a Walt Disney movie. They were just totally unrealistic and entirely out of keeping with the Trump style or the location they were meant to be in. DJT didn't immediately reject them, because he wanted to know what everyone else thought first. His negative impression might have been entirely wrong, and others may well have loved the plans. However, the response he got was always the same, from a wide variety of inputs: "This isn't right for the location or the brand." Everything—from the scale, the style, and the feel—changed dramatically, and the finished product sits so much better than it would have if we'd stuck to plan A.

People often obsess about a politician who changes a position on something. It seems our politicians are supposed to have all the answers now, be unwavering in their commitment, and never deviate from their path. That seems complete BS to me. How can you have all the answers all the time? Politicians are not superhuman, and they constantly find out new things that could—and should—alter their opinions. Shouldn't we encourage people to be flexible and capable of changing their stance depending on the evidence in front of them?

There's nothing wrong with that, and it's not a matter of inconsistency. You learn things along the way that affect how you think and make decisions. I'm not suggesting that you flip-flop all the time—you always need to be true to your mission—but instead that you be wise enough to recognize the value of a new path that can pay dividends and take you to your ultimate goal. Wouldn't you rather have a politician like that, than someone who is deadlocked and rigid?

As a fourteen-year resident of Trump World Tower, I can say from my own experience that people who live in the building love the place. When they wanted something more significant, they traded up and bought in the building. That's something rare in the ever-changing world of high-end New York condominiums, and it's achievable because Trump gave people what they wanted: excellent staff, great facilities, and beautiful spaces—and it's also the best investment you can think of.

The same happens with the golf course. Take the fifteenth hole in Aberdeen: we labored endlessly over whether to take the fairway around the dunes, toward the ocean, or to keep it inland, driving straight to the green. I can't tell you how many times, with different groups of people—golfers, non-golfers, architects, nonarchitects, journalists, residents, and golf pros—we asked for opinions, but ultimately, and for many different reasons, we decided to drive the hole straight, and it ended up being a unique, perfect hole that many people adore and comment on.

The exercise plays itself out on virtually every project where a decision is taken only after speaking to people with various perspectives.

There were so many different views on what we should have done with the lighthouse at Turnberry in South Ayrshire, Scotland, which is iconic and a significant site for the course because it sits between the ninth, tenth, and eleventh holes—one of the most dramatic series of links golf holes by the water. However, it also sits alongside the ruins of Turnberry Castle, where the legendary Scottish king Robert the Bruce was born in 1274. How incredible is that? Everyone had an opinion, from "Leave it alone" to "Renovate it," but it was Eric Trump who came up with the suggestion "Let's make it a halfway house." After a full restoration, it's now one of the most dramatic golf course restaurants in the world, with a beautiful luxury suite upstairs. It's so in demand that one person even rents it out for a week every month, he loves it that much.

Running for president had been in the back of Trump's mind for a very long time, and he asked everyone, everywhere, what they thought about it. There had been talk about him running for decades—and I know he'd publicly discussed it as long ago as the late 1980s, when, ironically, Oprah Winfrey had been a suggested running mate. At the time, he bought full-page political ads in some of the country's most prominent newspapers, which caused a storm of interest as to whether he was going to announce his candidacy. However, then, like now, he used that interest and base to express his frustration that the country was being kicked around by other nations and that he wanted to see America stand up for itself again. It seemed that he wasn't particularly pitching for the presidency, but it was clear that he didn't think it was such a crazy idea; the timing just wasn't right. The furor died down when he eventually poured cold water on the prospect of him running at that time, but it never truly went away.

The first time I heard him talk seriously about running for president was back in 2010–11. It was right in the middle of Obama's first term, and the country was divided over his effectiveness as president. The Democrats had just been crushed in the midterms, and the opportunity to put himself forward as a serious candidate was churning in DJT's head.

Quite a few people close to him pressed him to make the leap and run. Time and time again, Trump would come out on top in polling—and he was beating career politicians! He decided to wait; there was conflict in his head about whether to run and when. He knew that he could do it and do it well, but he also liked his life and what he was engaged in at that time.

However, the crowds kept trying to persuade him to run, and the suggestion seemed to be ever present wherever he went. When people are so openly rooting for you to go for the biggest job on the planet, it must make you take stock and think about whether you should give it a shot. However, Trump doesn't do things on the basis of just wanting to be in the race—he wants to win and win it well. When I went to see Roger Waters at Madison Square Garden with him around that time, as we walked in everyone was screaming for him to run, shouting, "President Trump." It was so surreal. He creates this incredible buzz wherever he goes, and love him or hate him, you can't ignore him. I don't ever remember people coming up to lambast him or have a go; they just wanted to see him, meet him, and shake his hand. They all wanted a picture with this global brand.

Everywhere he went, people were telling him to go for it and get rid of all the professional politicians who were running our country down. He was torn between his passion for doing what was needed for the benefit of the country and his realization that he would have to put his life's work—and his beloved business—to one side to make America great again. It would have been easy for him to walk away. He was already among the most admired people on the planet, enjoying his best years in business, and working closely with his kids and friends doing what he loved each and every day.

He's been accused of doing it for money or for attention. However, how much more famous could he be? Moreover, being president would rip him from his business and force him to close down some of his most lucrative opportunities. How could that possibly make him richer?

I can't tell you how many people he asked about his possible candidacy; he spoke to everyone about it. Trump has a tendency when he's weighing a question to look at it from so many different angles. He would ask, "What do you think of this?" and "What about that?" He wasn't just asking analysts or political advisers, he was asking lots of people he met in his day-to-day operations, from journalists to door attendants and waiters to his most senior confidants. He decided not to run in 2012, but there was something inside him—

and continuing public demand for him to give it a shot—that meant he pulled the trigger and ran as a Republican candidate in 2016.

It was carefully considered: a vision that he'd spent decades creating and years formulating correctly. He discussed it with so many people to seek their opinions and give him the likely positives and the negatives of putting himself in an even more high-profile position. Ultimately, of course, he was the one who made the final decision to run, but many people—and they know who they are—played a part in giving him the information he felt he needed to make his final choice.

As well as listening, the forty-fifth president of the United States of America is also incredibly keen at observing what's happening around him. If he's in a new environment, he likes to study what's going on in the surrounding area: What's the news in that area, what are people engaged with, what troubles them, what excites them, what's the critical arena of employment, and where has it succeeded and failed? He also loves to immerse himself in a new place by driving around to get a feel for it and to embrace the culture and mood. He loves to look at the architecture, see what businesses are on the main street, what restaurants are open, and whether the place is generally thriving or not. DJT observes people, reads the local papers wherever he is, and listens to everyone from the CEO to the doorman. He wants to drive around during the day and evening to get a feel for the place and its daytime and nighttime economy.

I remember once after having flown overseas, arriving early in the morning and working through the day, DJT wanted to get out at night and see the city. So after a dinner with prominent members of the local business community, he politely excused himself and grabbed the keys to a car and drove Keith and I around the bustling metropolis for about three hours—watching what was going on and noting where the economy was good and perhaps not so healthy. All this while driving on the wrong side of the road and having Keith and me with him passing comment!

Man, he doesn't miss a trick.

I would go check out clubs for him to see if they were operating at their best, or if they were thriving. He once said to me that there's stuff that's very difficult to teach—and luxury, the heart of our brand, is a good example: you either understand that or you don't. You can't teach it. You have to feel luxury. What makes something luxurious rather than gratuitous and ostentatious? There's a fine line, and sometimes people can't see that they've crossed it.

CHAPTER 15

The Man Who
Never Forgets

I t's fitting that DJT is a Republican, because he is like
an elephant: he never forgets," said Andy Kjos, the links
superintendent at West Palm Beach. Andy has seen DJT's
prodigious memory recall for himself.

Every spring on his last trip to Florida for the season, usually around Easter, Trump would say, "Andy! Let's take a ride
around the course." So they would ride around, and Trump
pointed out things he wanted to be done over the summer
once it closed. There could be some fundamental things, and
there would usually be a couple of big projects, because he

always wanted to give the members something new for the next season. Andy took a few notes down whenever he could, and it was fast paced and intense, but DJT didn't write a thing down, not one note—ever.

"The first year after the first ride-around I went to my office to go through my notes and make sure I didn't forget anything," Andy remembered. "The rides were intense, and when he said something, he meant it! They were not suggestions.

"I'll never forget my first summer, a few months after the first end-of-the-season ride with DJT, I got a call in July—and it was DJT. 'Andy! How's the golf course?' I gave him a few updates, and then he started going through our ride like it was yesterday. I was like, 'Holy crap! He doesn't take one note, yet he is going down the list I made like it was right in front of him.'"

It was at this point that Andy learned that when DJT says something, do it right away and don't think he will forget. The detail of his memory is extraordinary.

"We would go through, hole by hole, over the phone in great detail: 'Put three six-foot coconut trees on the right side of hole four, twenty-five yards before the first bunker on the right next to the lake and stagger them in a triangle pattern. You have to use an odd number of trees, Andy, never an even number; odd numbers of trees look better, an even number of trees never looks as good.' We would go through the course hole by hole like this in great detail." Superintendents learn to visualize the course and can do this very well. However, it is impressive for an owner to know a course as well as a superintendent, given how much less time the owner is there.

In the fall, DJT would return around Thanksgiving, and

sure enough, he would go over the list he and Andy had made in the spring like it was yesterday. "The man doesn't forget!" Andy said. His people have to carry out what he wants, and if he doesn't see it's getting done he quite rightly isn't impressed—and the ramifications can be severe!

Mike Vergara, the senior vice president of design and construction who started his working life as a chef, knows he has to get everything perfect to ensure DJT is content. Mike managed the massive $200 million overhaul of the Old Post Office (or OPO, as we all call it) in Washington, DC.

Mike had labored hard with Ivanka, Eric, and DJT himself and was working crazy hours and driving a punishing schedule to get the place open and running on time and on budget. This guy is incredibly focused—he even came in under budget, which is almost unheard of for a project of this scale—but the pressure never stopped.

Just weeks before the official opening in 2016—a soft opening—it was at the height of DJT running for president. To be honest, Mike thought that Trump would have way too many things to worry about other than the OPO opening, but no, he never let his attention wane from the incredible project that was the restoration of that magnificent building.

Trump had obviously been there regularly, and early on in the project, he'd noticed a glitch in the restoration of one of the windows on the eighth floor. The restoration was already proving a costly and complicated process because it had to meet all the standards required on a project of this historical importance and magnitude. Mike and Steve Dalton, a consultant on the project, were standing with him at these historic windows. Remember, this is a massive contract, because there were so many windows, and they had to be perfect. Mr. Trump knew that the window was completed and had been signed off as being perfect despite there being an obvious flaw. In effect, the reflective quality of the glass within the frame was just not as good as it should have been—and was obvious to anyone who looked carefully, but especially to DJT.

He spent an hour in a meeting and then just at the end he called Steve over and asked, "Steve, how is the window guy doing?" It was a relatively innocuous question, and Steve said he was doing really good. It was the moment DJT was waiting for. He said, "Do you think this is really good?" and pointed out the deficiency in the glass' reflective covering, knowing that the old window was now itself encapsulated in modern glass.

Mike remembered the fallout: "He was furious that this had been passed as of the necessary standard, but, thankfully, I managed to step in and tell him that the safety glass was being removed the very next day to ensure the deficiency could be fixed."

Fast-forward to the official opening, and Mike hadn't seen Trump for at least a year because he'd been on the campaign trail. It was an incredible day, with so many dignitaries and VIPs in attendance.

"I greeted him and Ivanka, and he said, 'Great to see you, Mike,' and he slapped me on the shoulder, shook my hand, and said, 'Have you fixed those windows yet?'

"I remember swearing and saying, 'I can't believe you asked that!' We had a good laugh about it, but only because I had fixed them, thankfully! However, that's just him."

Trump is a perfectionist who never forgets an instruction he's given—and he knows what's required. "Some people thrive on it, and others can't cope—but I love it," Mike said, thankfully.

I have seen that level of detail on so many occasions. However, more recently, when Trump took my great friend and coauthor Damian Bates and me on a tour of Lincoln's bedroom in the White House. He gave us a historic blow-by-blow account of everything in the room so that when I walked out, I felt that it was almost as if Lincoln had a fourth seat at the table at dinner that night. He explained the whole story of Lincoln's rise to prominence and his very special and preserved place at the White House and the tragedy that befell him when his son Willie died in childhood—aged just eleven—due to what was believed to have been typhoid fever, which was very common in Washington at the time.

It was incredible to listen to the narrative Trump told us, and he was genuinely somber with his comments. "The tragedy that President Lincoln suffered was unimaginable," he said. "And the melancholy he suffered as a consequence stayed with him for years. Can you imagine the pain he was in? Tragic, just tragic."

There was an air of sadness and stillness in the room, the room where Lincoln had stood at the end of that beautiful rosewood bed, looked down at his son's lifeless body, and said, "My poor boy, he was too good for this earth. God has called him home. I know that he is much better off in heaven, but then we loved him so. It is hard, hard to have him die!"

President Trump sighed, turned on his heels, and beckoned for us to leave the room to its sadness and ghosts.

CHAPTER 16

Surviving the Blasts

Short of my parents, no one has done more for my career than Donald J. Trump. He entrusted me with projects that he was passionate about, and I will always have tremendous gratitude for those experiences. It's very much part of the person I've grown to be. And I know many others feel the same, both inside and outside the organization.

Oren Kattan is a case in point.

He's a Miami-raised landscape genius who got his big break when his path crossed Mr. Trump's. Oren had worked in textiles and had branched out—excuse the pun—into landscaping, then started undertaking work for the Trump

Org. He's an incredible American with a background as an Iraqi Jew.

"They knew I hadn't done anything bigger than small commercial jobs and domestic landscaping," Oren said. "I didn't know anything about golf and had never played a round of golf in my life. However, [Trump] gave me a chance and I know I scored a ten for the landscaping work I did at Doral."

As well as completely renovating the landscape at Trump National Doral Miami and other venues, Oren and his company, LUSHlife, have worked in Washington planting trees inside the fantastic renovation of the Old Post Office, at Trump International Golf Club, West Palm Beach, and at Mar-a-Lago.

Oren spent five years working on various projects with Trump, who came around every week and chatted. Oren had his cell phone number to call him whenever there was an issue. "It always struck me that when we talked he would say the difference between experience and talent is that experience is lazy, talent never gives up," Oren recalled.

Trump was also very interested in the people who were working for him and Oren. He would chat with them and find out their views, and he gave them the respect they deserved no matter where they were from. "I'd heard of his reputation before I started working for him—that he would screw the little guy to get precisely what he wanted," Oren said. "But I found a guy I could work with and who treated me with the greatest respect and wanted me to go places. I found people—both working for the organization and as contractors—who had been with him for twenty and thirty years. People don't work with you and follow you for that period if you're just out to screw them all the time."

DJT wasn't in it for the plaudits, of course, and he'd expect hard work and returns on his investment, and he always wanted to get the best deal he could. However, I can roll off a number of companies that have gone on to secure incredible contracts with other clients because of the work they did for DJT.

Few people who have more responsibility and day-to-day commitments than the president of the United States, but Trump still makes time to keep in touch with me. If I'm ever in Washington or when he's in Palm Beach, I can call him up, and if he's got the time over the next few days, he'll ask me to swing by to say hi. They're always quick, simple chats, but he remains loyal and connected to his associates. It'd be very easy to forget about a guy like me in the rough-and-tumble of Washington, DC, but it's a measure of the man that he wants to keep in touch with people like me, people he can trust. I don't always agree with some of his actions and methods, but I still have great respect for him and feel that our relationship was built on that trust. As I came to realize, he frequently was right—that's just how it was.

As a person who has been accused of having a legendary temper myself on occasion, I understand that sometimes in life it's okay to get a little angry. In my mind, if you can't get mad and show some rage from time to time, you're living a sorry life. If you're passionate about something, then sometimes it's okay to get angry, and this certainly wasn't an exception with Mr. Trump! As anyone who has been on the receiving end of that anger knows, it's a terrible place to be at the time, but there's usually a valid reason behind the response.

No one can perhaps reflect that better than Andy Kjos,

the superintendent at Trump International Golf Club in West Palm Beach. "I learned a lot my first year as a twenty-eight-year-old superintendent working for DJT, but by far the most valuable lesson I learned was, 'Don't trim any trees unless DJT tells you to,'" Andy said, shaking his head.

"Trump International Golf Club is lined with oak trees, and I swear DJT knows every one of them. Standard practice with these types of oaks is that they need to be pruned to maintain their proper shape and structure in a formal landscape. Some trees if not appropriately pruned will become structurally weak, and when a storm comes, they'll be far more likely to break apart and be destroyed.

"I brought in a certified arborist, and we went through tree by tree, pruning what needed to be done," Andy recalled. "The work was performed, and the trees looked great. Some trees had what one might call 'aggressive cuts,' but they had never been pruned, and it had needed to be done in order to make them safe and able to thrive." Well, what Andy learned the next season when DJT returned was that "necessary pruning" is a relative term. "Andy! Get in the cart, let's look at the course." Trump got in the cart, and they checked out the course, and everything was going great.

Near the end of the ride coming up to hole eighteen, DJT seemed very happy with the condition of the course and loved the changes that had been made. Andy felt pretty good about himself, and then it happened.

"He very abruptly stopped the cart and pointed to a small oak between the fourteenth and eighteenth holes and asked, 'Did you cut a branch off that tree?' Very proud of the work we did last summer I said, 'Yes sir, we trimmed all the oak trees,' and this is where everything went wrong.

"He said, 'You did what? You did this to all the oaks?' I said, 'Yes, sir,' then the cart took off like a rocket, bussing around the course looking at all the oak trees, and I heard language that would make a sailor blush. It was the longest ten minutes of my life."

DJT wasn't happy, and despite Andy trying to explain the process, and why it had been done, DJT wasn't having any of it. Andy winced as he recalled one particularly tough moment: "The line I will never forget him saying to me was, 'If I cut your arm off, would that make you stronger?'"

It didn't end there either. Trump went back to Mar-a-Lago, and he was telling people what Andy had done and that he wanted to throw him in the ocean. Andy got a call later that night from Mar-a-Lago, and he could tell from the secretary's voice on the other end that this was not going to be good. He was on hold for a couple of seconds, and then DJT came on the line, and the berating continued. Andy got the arborist who did the work on the phone, but there was no appeasing DJT.

"I learned a precious lesson that day I will never, ever forget: you can do great work, and you may even be right, but if you don't communicate it effectively, your ship is sunk before it even leaves the harbor.

"I also learned you have to be tough—they don't teach you toughness in school, but I learned very early on, if you are going to make it in this business, you have to be tough enough to take extreme criticism and learn from it and not wilt under pressure." The reality of business is that passionate people are going to yell at you, not because they don't like you, but because they want the best; they want success.

Andy thought for sure he was going to be fired. "I felt so bad; I had never made anyone that mad in my life, but somehow he decided not to fire me. I like to think he realized that the effort I had put into the course made the difference, but the fact he flew back to New York and didn't return to Florida for a couple of weeks is what probably saved my job."

Later that year, Trump joked with members in front of Andy that "Andy cost me a million dollars in oak trees, but he is doing a good job with the grass, so we will keep him around."

"That line broke that ice between us, but to this day he will still give me grief for trimming those trees—sixteen years later! The man doesn't forget."

Of course, Trump knows the science behind the practice of pruning branches and the fact that it stimulates better growth in trees. However, he specifically uses hard-hitting words and sometimes will make a point through a shocking example to have the greatest impact on the listener and make a point that he or she won't ever forget.

And look how Andy never forgot!

You only have to watch one of his rallies to see how those methods still serve him well in the political arena.

I remember when we were in Doonbeg in Ireland (Trump International Golf Links and Hotel) when Trump shredded me. Mr. Trump had an evident vision for the changes he wanted making at that complex, a beautiful development designed by the fantastic golfer Greg Norman that overlooks the Atlantic on the west coast of Ireland. Trump was irate—he wanted an area of mounding to occur at the right-hand side of the driving range. There were various issues that we had to make choices about, and we as a team collectively believed there were other, more pressing matters to attend to—one was to either deal with the mounding that DJT wanted focus on or create mounds in the back, where there was an exposed internal road that used to cause golfers irritation when cars and trucks drove by. Myself; our architect, Dr. Martin Hawtree; and the guys on site decided the first thing we would do was mound that area out back, and the rest could follow later.

When Trump turned up, he exploded.

He didn't take issue that we all agreed that the mounding at the back of the site should be first. No, that wasn't the problem at all. He was enraged that we hadn't listened to him and had gone off and done our own thing. He had been clear in his instructions, and he wanted them followed. I was responsible in his eyes. I was in charge, and therefore it was clearly my fault. He let me have it, and it was an awkward conversation that took place in front of many people.

It was a reminder that I had to listen to him, and it was a reminder that I've never forgotten. You don't make a decision on something he cares deeply about without explaining it to him first. Many of his critics have focused on his temper, but in actuality, it is a useful tool to convey his passion about his point—and, trust me, on this occasion, the message was received loud and clear. For me, I knew that his anger would be short lived, and I just didn't let it bother me too much. If I accepted the responsibility, there would be no grudges, and the air would be quickly cleared. I thought that was a much better way of dealing with business than holding grudges and festering over it. Shout, scream, deal with it, get over it, and move on. To succeed in life, you have to be able to handle conflict.

People need to be told unequivocally, "I'm not happy with this," and if you need a tongue-lashing, you face up to it for a few minutes, take your medicine, and move on. However, that is one of the endearing things about Trump: you take the criticism, accept it, learn from it, and move on. No one is doing you any favors in life if you can't take the bullet and accept it.

The world is often a savage and brutal place, and you have to be ready for it. The real sense of safety comes from knowing you are on a unified team, one with the same goals—not from avoiding criticism when you're wrong.

However, don't think that DJT is shouting and bawling all the time. Nothing could be further from the truth; most often, he's a measured and calm person. Even if he thinks you are wrong, he's always willing to listen. However, like a true leader, he makes the decision that he feels and believes is right. I know that people are surprised at how he stops, listens to what they have to say, and processes that. From the guest having a drink at the bar of his hotel to the doormen showing him in, he's fascinated about what they think and what can be done to make things better and improve on the offerings already there.

It's not just me saying that.

Andy Billick is now construction manager for the Trump Org, but he was a finishing carpenter at Bedminster when

DJT was applying the finishing touches to this fantastic development project. Andy was in the ballroom as they were finishing off the woodwork, and Mr. Trump swept in as two huge decorative cabinets, curios that stretched almost from the floor to the ceiling, were brought in. It took a team of guys hours to bring them in without bashing anything, and they were struggling and huffing and puffing.

Andy said, "The cabinets were so out of place in there—it was a ballroom and they were the sort of things that you would see in a posh dining room to display the best china that you had. Elsewhere in the hotel, it would have been fine, but they looked terrible there."

Trump asked everyone, "What do you think? Don't they look great?" Everyone was saying, "Yeah, they're amazing." They all thought they were horrible but couldn't bring themselves to say it, and they all agreed with him until Trump came to Andy.

"Now, I've always said that I would tell him the truth, and I've stuck to that. He grabbed me, and I said, 'I think it looks ridiculous.' The look on the faces of the managers was a picture. DJT looked at me, and he said, 'You're right, that's the answer I was looking for! Why did no one say anything? Get them out of here!'

"The managers were cursing me because [the cabinets] took forever to get in and they'd take forever to get out again! He asked me what I thought we should put there in the place of these huge cabinets and I said, 'Put mirrors in there because you're surrounded by glass, and they'll be amazing; you can bring the outside in.'

"He said it was a fabulous idea and that's what we did."

So Andy did the one thing that DJT wants more than anything: for people to call it as they see it. He gave an honest opinion, even though it had contradicted what DJT had initially wanted to do. It's a common misconception about DJT: that he doesn't change his mind. Of course he does; a smart guy will see things evolve and is prepared to be persuaded of his need to do things a different way. He never stops, never gives up, and always wants to make things move on, improve, and take them to a new level.

Andy's honesty would raise his profile in the company, and he was later put in charge of some of our most prestigious projects, including the renovation of the stunning Turnberry hotel in South Ayrshire, Scotland.

CHAPTER 17

Trust and Failure

The Trump Organization has a uniquely high level of trust, which exists from the top down. The business consists of a very small but tightly knit group of people who depend on each other and yet are still able to achieve a global footprint. While talent, hard work, and perseverance were undoubtedly major components to the organization's success, in retrospect, the trust factor was the most significant.

It's Trump's vision that an employee is ultimately charged with turning into reality, but any authority, his voice, was delegated from him. He would say, "I'm giving you the tools, the guidance, and the support to get in there and make your own decisions, but it's my vision that's going to be executed."

Not a day went by that I wasn't proud to be a part of the operation in Scotland. Some of the happiest moments of my career were spent on the project with DJT, Don Jr., Sarah Malone, and the rest of the development team. I still get that sense of pride every time someone writes or calls me to express how much fun he or she had on the site.

Sarah was there running the development team and the whole operation day in and day out. She was the person on the ground who was really making decisions and gathering the information, and ultimately, DJT had to trust her ability to read things objectively and provide him—three thousand miles away—with unbiased, clean information.

Your decisions are only as good as the information you rely on, and you need to trust people to provide you with straight, uncorrupted facts, or else you're throwing darts at a target with a blindfold on. Once you have trust in the flow of information, you can introduce the concept of loyalty. People tend to perform better when they know that they're trusted and respected, with headquarters equally able to rely on information being provided. When that virtuous circle is complete, people tend to perform beyond expectations—if they also genuinely love what they're doing—because they're acting out of a sense of pride and enjoyment, rather than because they need to make a living.

Those are two very different drivers.

There's a big difference between being happy and enjoying what you do, and logging in the hours and waiting for your next paycheck. Sure, we all need to earn the dollars to enable us to pay the bills at the end of the month, but I always look on my career with The Trump Organization more as a lifestyle than a job. Of course, it still is a job, and there needs to be a clear separation between your personal and family time and what you do in your career. We all know people who have given everything to their professional development at the expense of their family, never having seen their kids grow up or having sacrificed so much that the family becomes estranged. That's gotta be tough, and, invariably, getting that delicate balance correct is incredibly challenging, but my overall mentality is that the role I carry out is as much a lifestyle as it is a job—but it's a lifestyle I'm happy with.

It's different from the guy who clocks in and does his eight hours and clocks out. Anyone who has read any of DJT's books or heard his speeches has heard him say directly that you have to love what you do or you'll never be successful. He's the epitome of that.

Every president goes golfing, or to luxury retreats, and every minute of that time is still filled with work. When Trump became president, he was already in that mode. He didn't have to adjust to turning golf trips into negotiations and plane rides into briefings. He works 24/7, and there's no separation between recreation time and business.

You have to find something you love doing, and you'll do it well, and you'll go through life with a positive attitude because you're doing something you want to rather than something you have to. I can speak only for myself, but I have lived it both ways. I've had jobs that I just clocked in and out of and couldn't wait to leave at the end of the day. It didn't mean I didn't do the work well, because I wanted to perform well, but I go back to Aberdeen now, and although I hadn't done anything like that before, I knew that I loved it. I was helping build something great in the country where my mother was from and where I have family.

There were many days and issues on which we butted heads, and I did spend many days in the proverbial doghouse when I made a decision Trump didn't agree with—and for the record, we did clash over some issues. For example, I thought we often gave our most vocal critics—and people who had no real standing or legitimate beef against us—too much oxygen of publicity. My view was that often such critics were better ignored than engaged with. However, Mr. Trump has an underlying desire to show people why he is right and they are wrong. It isn't anything to do with bravado or ego; he genuinely feels that if he is strong in his conviction, others need to see it. If he ever left alone an issue or the source of a conflict, it would frequently disappear in a flash, but by engaging with it, he merely gave his critics a platform to respond and to continue burning the fire.

I'm not suggesting for one minute that people shouldn't have the right to express their opinions or even fight us over a good cause, but many of Trump's critics were small-minded malcontents who merely wanted to give him a bloody nose— and we gave them the opportunity to do it. Some people were hacks and professional agitators who lived their lives objecting to one issue or another, and they couldn't believe their luck when we decided to take them on and explain why we thought they were wrong. To them, it was free publicity. They had engaged with one of the biggest names on the planet, and it merely emboldened them and made them seem important.

We ended up causing ourselves more harm and creating more work and headaches because we chose to engage with this motley crew of agitators, instead of just ignoring their petty criticisms and issues.

However, Trump has a core belief that if he's sure he's right, he has to try to impress his case on people. It's a sense of wanting to show people that his argument is correct and that they can be persuaded of that cause. Sometimes people agree with him, and sometimes they don't. I told him that I didn't agree with this approach and that we should know when to engage and when to leave critics alone to avoid causing ourselves more trouble. In his defense, it was just another example of how much he cares and how hard he works; everything needed a response, and every element had to be examined. So although not responding and not engaging was probably the best way to handle such situations, he wanted every angle covered, and it became a blessing and a curse.

I remember that the night after the Aberdeen project was rejected, he said, "Don't worry, take a breath, and regroup tomorrow." The next day he called me up, and he had read the word "devastated" in an interview that I'd given. To DJT, that word sounds like the speaker is curled up in a corner somewhere and is finished. He said you should instead always be ready to fight.

He had that never-quit philosophy—he would fight to the last breath. Do not quit; if you have a setback, stand up and take another step forward.

CHAPTER 18

Why I Work for Donald J. Trump

arah Malone stood up from behind her desk and walked over to shut the door to her office to ensure she had no interruptions. Spread across her desk, in this incredibly picturesque part of Scotland, lay vast renderings of planned housing and future master plans for the estate that Trump has so meticulously envisioned to be his legacy.

Clocks showing the time in the United Kingdom, New York City, and Los Angeles bedeck the walls. Sarah returned to her seat and smiled. "Nothing prepares you for working with The Donald. I've watched the most seasoned professionals, politicians, and leading minds fold in his presence. His style, his thought process, and his actions dumbfound people."

Sarah knows that for the uninitiated, Trump's methods may appear madness. *You can't say that. You can't do that!* She stopped and paused to think how best to describe his style and why it may throw people entirely off kilter.

"The blunt, simplistic, and unscripted frankness of Trump's rhetoric belies the complexity of his character and skill," she said. As executive vice president of his assets in the northeast of Scotland, she reported directly to the man himself and knows him better than most. "He outflanks the best of the best, not with fancy words or complex strategic maneuvers but by stealth, instinct, ruthlessness, and boundless belief. With Trump, anything is possible if you believe," Sarah said.

A call came in, and she immediately swooped to pick up the line as Eric Trump looked for an update on the current planning process. Architectural blueprints, drawings, maps, and spreadsheets were strewn across the conference table, the office jam-packed with files spanning years of development history. Comfortable and bright—and roughly about the same square footage as Eric's office in NYC—this unassuming space is the engine room of Trump's beloved project in Scotland. Trees swayed in the early spring sunshine outside. The noise and chaos of New York are a long, long way away from the quiet and solitude of Aberdeen, Scotland—more than three thousand miles, to be precise.

Sarah is a battle-hardened warrior in The Trump Organization. She's faced the vagaries of dozens of politicians from all strata who sought to block her path in getting the golf development up and running. She's also been bombarded by myriad protesters—some reasoned, many fundamental in their hatred for The Donald—who did everything they could to make her life, both personal and professional, as difficult as possible, even going so far as to abuse her over her looks and spit, literally, in her face.

However, Sarah is not beaten or downtrodden, just determined to get the job done—precisely as Trump knew she would be. Sarah believes that more often than not our political figures tell us what they think we want or need to hear, describing the "narratives that are designed to appease many and offend few," as she put it.

That's not how Trump operates. Sarah picked up after her phone call: "Trump is not constrained by conventions or the standard rules of engagement. He doesn't dance to the beat of anyone's drum. He sets his own stage—it's his rules—his way."

That's not to say that Sarah didn't find it challenging trying to adapt to that approach when she first started with the company. "I had to completely change my way of thinking when I entered Trump's inner circle. All bets were off. This was another world, where fear has no place."

She received the phone call out of the blue from the office of Donald J. Trump ten years ago. That call changed her life. Her secretary at the time promised it wasn't a ruse and urged her to take the call from New York. "I wondered why on earth Trump wanted to speak to me," Sarah remembered. "I was knee-deep in battle-armaments and antique militaria!"

It was me on the other end of the line, calling on behalf of Trump himself to offer congratulations on her recent endeavors and to request a meeting.

She said she will never forget strolling down Fifth Avenue, heading to Trump Tower, some time later, to meet the legend in person. Expectant and a little apprehensive, if not somewhat bemused as to how she found herself in this situation, Sarah reflected on the pending meeting with a global real estate mogul. "Why bother meeting me? Get someone else to do it, right?"

For the thirty-four-year-old woman museum director, this was not a typical day. In her own words, he'd plucked her out of obscurity, relatively speaking. "Sitting behind his desk, Trump lifted his eyes and invited me to take a seat. No sooner had I entered the room, and the fateful question came booming from his lips: 'What do you know about golf, Sarah Malone?'" she recalled, laughing. Surely he knew that wasn't her arena—what the blazes was she doing there?

"I wasn't about to bullshit Donald Trump. He must have met every chancer in the game, and I certainly wasn't about to become the next.

"'I don't know anything about golf, Mr. Trump.' I barely knew my tee from green, and I'm honest if nothing else." She admitted she did take an extended trip to St Andrews—the home of golf, and a couple of hours' drive from Aberdeen—to educate herself on all things pertaining to the game, both past and present, before heading to New York, but she wasn't about to bluff it.

"Trump laughed at my response and the conversation flowed."

They talked UK politics, the state of the economy, business, and his planned investment in Scotland. He asked about what made her tick and what she loved to do. All the while,

Sarah recalled how she soaked up the vibe from the epicenter of the Trump empire: executives popping in and out, *The Apprentice* ratings and plaudits being yelled from the doorways, and every inch of the office crammed with glossy front pages, signed sporting memorabilia from American greats, and row after row of family pictures. His desk was notably piled high with newspapers and magazines.

Trump illuminated her on how she'd come to be there.

Several months earlier, he'd read a large article on her, one that featured HRH the Duke of Rothesay (otherwise known as Prince Charles) and a significant building and renovation project she'd completed in Scotland. It appeared that the next in line for the crown, one of the finest regiments in British military history, and an award from Her Majesty the Queen had caught his attention.

Even now Sarah seemed to think it all a bit surreal. She leaned back in her chair, and her eyes turned to the heavens as she remembered a time before Trump. "I was a strong woman working in a male-dominated environment: former generals, serving soldiers, and everything in between. Battle strategy and firearms were my language. I knew my AK-47 from my SA80. I'd taken a sleepy museum with a long military history and helped transform it, making it relevant to this generation and financially secure for the future."

Frankly, to Sarah, she was the least obvious choice for her last career move, let alone this one, but she'd flourished against the odds. Trump got it. It seemed he saw that fighting spirit in Sarah Malone, too.

"I think you've been at the museum long enough, Sarah Malone. You should come work for me. We often pluck people out of other disciplines," he elaborated at that first meeting. "That's what we do. What do you say?" There it was. How do you turn down Trump, let alone a life-changing job opportunity to work on a history-making project on your home turf? She believed his investment would transform the leisure and tourism industry Sarah was so passionate about.

This had nothing to do with being a subject specialist. Trump was looking for strength of character. A local to lead from the front. "You can be my hands and feet on the ground," he declared. Trump appointed her executive vice president of his property in Scotland that day.

"Congratulations, Sarah Malone." (He has always referred to Sarah by her full name, for some reason known only to him.) "I want you to be everywhere, know everyone, do everything, and do a great job. And you don't need to worry about playing golf." Sarah vividly remembered Trump's words reverberating around his office, high up in the New York skyline.

That was the brief. That was her job description. As she put it, it was for her to mess it up. Before she left his office, Trump reflected on the newspaper article that had grabbed his initial interest, and he laughed heartily. "You know, Sarah Malone, your story was printed on the opposite page from mine, and I asked myself, 'Who is this woman? She even has a bigger photograph than me!'"

Sarah laughed at the memory. "From the get-go, Trump always had a sense of humor."

She reflected on those early years: "As a global entrepreneur, Trump personally headhunting me didn't make much sense at the time, but having worked with him for many years, I've come to realize that he relies heavily on his gut instincts and discernment of people and their motives."

Sarah knows that Trump is prepared to get down and dirty and into the details to ensure things are done right. He didn't send someone else in to find the right project manager; he did it himself.

I later explained that DJT had been tracking her profile in the press for months. The Trump Organization had made some calls to get the measure of her before his secretary even lifted the phone. She'd been well and truly vetted, it seemed.

"Little did I know that the project he'd embarked upon on British soil would turn out to be so adversarial." Sarah smiled. "My role had little to do with sport and was everything to do with people, principles, and politics. Trump knew precisely what he was doing. For those who knew me, my seemingly soft media profile veiled my steely nature. I was no pushover."

Before joining the firm, she'd dealt with the media for over fifteen years and for the most part been treated with respect. However, before she was even on the Trump payroll, the shift was meteoric. "Overnight the press turned," she recalled. "I hadn't even had a chance to digest the opportunity ahead, let alone make a major blunder, when the wolves set upon me.

"After my first press conference alongside Don Trump Jr. and George, the first day's papers went from passable to brutal. The jaws of hell appeared to have opened. I was stitched up, lied about, and portrayed as a fraudster. It was horrific. My worst nightmare. It takes years to earn your stripes and build a reputation—and seconds for the scurrilous daily tabloids to rob you of it. I felt sick."

What the hell was she going to say to Trump? Sarah felt that her first media conference on his behalf had been a hatchet job.

Trump called her later that day. "I've seen the papers. Don't worry about it, and don't go changing. You're like me. We're going to build great things together."

That was a watershed moment, what she described as a salutary experience. "I learned a great deal about the company and the man that day; it was part of my baptism of fire. I soon came to realize this was the norm."

However, being a woman working for Trump was never going to be a piece of cake when the media—and some cruel protesters—got their teeth into her.

"Call me anytime, Sarah Malone." That's what Trump told her.

He couldn't possibly mean *any*time, could he? It came as a great surprise to her that Trump did indeed mean "anytime." Calls directly to his apartment, his home, in Trump Tower in the early hours of the morning, were frequent. With a five-hour time difference, Sarah's day was in full swing when New York was just waking up. She was always conscious of intruding on his family time and his private space, and on many occasions, the phone was lifted by Melania. "She was just so gracious, kind, and engaging," Sarah said. "I've always marveled at her modest, gentle disposition. She is unquestionably the most elegant and unassuming woman I have ever met." They have a clear rapport—and probably some of it is forged by the constant attacks for being important women in Trump's orbit.

Trump was always very responsive. He never missed a call

or forgot to ring back. Strangely, irrespective of what he was doing, she never felt brushed off or that he didn't have time. He always made you feel that you were his priority.

Sarah knows that Trump's an incredibly complex person— "One minute he's operating at 100,000 feet in the air, the next he's absorbed in the most myopic of detail. He doesn't shun the small stuff." For this Scottish EVP, his capacity for information and making decisions large and small is extraordinary. "His energy puts most of us to shame. I've seen him charge across hundred-foot dunes while most of us, panting and breathless, lag far behind. When he's on a mission, the creativity, positivity, and determination are intoxicating. His ability to motivate and inspire others is unmatched."

Despite his powerhouse persona, Sarah believes he can also be incredibly kind. Trump—and his whole family, for that matter—have been supportive in good times and bad, through marriage, babies, and poor health. She is adamant that while he may be brutal in business, he cares about people, especially his people.

Sarah recalled one occasion when Trump was due to attend a significant parliamentary hearing in the United Kingdom and had an intense schedule ahead of him. Sarah knew this because she'd drafted it. As soon as he landed on British soil, her phone rang. She'd been hospitalized a few days earlier. It was critical at the time but not life threatening, more of a shock to her and her family. Trump called her cell—she was propped up in a hospital bed—and she could hear the 757 engines in the background.

He'd quite literally just landed and was standing on the tarmac. "I'm okay. I'm okay. I'm fine, seriously, I will be fine," Sarah told him. She was always there to greet him on arrival, and he knew she had to be very sick not to be there. In typical Trump fashion, he questioned her confidence in the medical care she was receiving, drilling her on the detail until she had to shut him down.

"We were on one hell of a journey at that time. A mission that centered on four miles of coastline along the northeast of Scotland. Trump had seen potential in a piece of land that we natives had ignored, neglected even.

"For me, this is one of the hallmarks of the man: He sees what others overlook. He goes where others dare not." Sarah is utterly convinced of his tremendous vision and his ability for getting things done.

However, it doesn't come without a challenge. "During my long tenure with Trump," Sarah said, "the one thing I have come to realize is that the bigger the vision you have, the bigger the opposition you'll encounter. One is commensurate with the other."

She stood up and walked across her office to take a seat at the conference table and began to flick through the future plans for the site. She described how so often in life and business, people sit neatly in their comfort zones, easing themselves along the road according to what they are ready for or what they perceive they can handle. However, with Trump, it's the direct opposite. "With The Donald, I can safely say that you abandon all rules, safety nets, comfort zones, and all hedge betting—it's all or nothing, do or die. If he's in, he's in, and he's in to win."

Trump International Golf Links in Scotland was and is a visionary project. It brought a whole host of challenges with it, and she's personally had to dig very deep to navigate the endless trip wires, hazards, and obstacles that have been thrown at the project. Sarah recalled how when Trump's interest in the property was ignited, all he heard was how impossible it would be to build there, how it couldn't be done and it would cost too much, even if he did manage to penetrate the red tape. She knew the coastline well. She'd played on the beaches as a child. This was her patch. The scale of the dunes and the drama of the North Sea is sensational, but no one had ever seen them as special. No one ever paid them any attention, few people visited them, and very few cared. It was a vast stretch of beach on which to walk the dog, but that was about the size of it.

That was, until Trump came to town.

"We'd never heard of anyone contemplating doing what he was proposing to do. However, that's Trump all over. He had a tremendous vision for the site that both excited and stunned the Scottish people," Sarah said matter-of-factly.

"Until he declared his interest in the dunes, no one gave a dicky bird. Then, out of the woodwork, the naysayers started to emerge; a handful of environmental zealots claimed it was of geomorphic interest and Trump became public enemy number one," she said.

The battle had begun.

For the next five years, Trump spent millions on environmental studies, assessments, and analyses. He hired the leading minds in the country and knew more about the dunes than any statutory ecological body in the land. Sarah said these bodies relied on Trump's reports to fight their corner. The perversity of the situation still baffles her today.

Hurdle after hurdle, she and the team persevered and pressed ahead. Finally, the economic case for development was won, and, as she puts it, "no dune before or since has been afforded so much attention or investment."

Trump made it clear he was going to create the world's greatest golf course, a world-class destination for golfers from around the world. To Sarah in this quiet corner of Scotland that was known more for its oil and gas exploration than its tourism potential, this was great economic news. The journey to that end has, however, been fraught with challenge.

More than forty planning applications, twenty-four planning hearings, a parliamentary hearing and a full public inquiry, countless public consultations, an arrest (not a member of the Trump camp), an admission to a psychiatric unit (yes, that's correct), several court cases, including one with an elderly lady who lived in a camper, a multimillion-pound court case over wind turbines, a national dustup with the BBC, and a three-year spat with the former first minister of Scotland was just for starters. Sarah was almost breathless as she reeled off the list of hurdles. Shaking her head, she suggested that you could be excused for thinking that Trump was planning to build a nuclear waste site, not planting grass, such was the noise that ensued.

Along the way, she has been mocked, vilified, scorned, tripped up, stitched up, and even spat at, all because—as Sarah sees it—a US developer was committed to spending hundreds of millions on the local economy. "I have felt ashamed of my kin and, frankly, it made me even more resolute to fight every single small-minded, self-serving agenda that was thrown our way."

This lady is feisty and doesn't give up—just like her boss. "Trump has the extraordinary ability to overcome anything," Sarah said. "I've looked at seemingly insurmountable obstacles only to look back at them in the distance years later. The man is a force to be reckoned with. He sets his face against the opposition and plows ahead to get the job done."

Forget those who throw stones from their armchairs or hide behind their keyboards. Sarah believes that anyone who takes the time actually to see what Trump has built and to understand the journey, the obstacles he was forced to overcome, cannot help but give him credit. Even if that's grudging credit.

And the investment continues.

She's watched hardened critics swallow their pride and admit he's built one of the greatest golf courses of all time. For her, like him or loathe him, Trump delivers. To Sarah this was never a battle of golf versus sand dunes; it was a battle of big vision versus no vision. Sarah shook her head once again and sighed. "Since when is sand more important than the creations of jobs, prosperity, and opportunities for people?"

The press spun it as a tale of the little guy versus the big guy. However, for Sarah and her loyal team continuing to push DJT's vision, this was about challenging head on the pervading mind-set in her part of the world that you "can't do." "Trump is an opponent of the status quo. The man shook the very system that was holding the country back. That's why I work for him," she declared coolly.

"I respect him and his candor. He's not fake. What you see is what you get. You know where you stand with Trump. You know whether you are friend or foe."

They say all is fair in love and war. With Trump, never a truer word was spoken. Those are the rules he plays by.

Sarah remembered one evening, in a chauffeur-driven car en route to dinner, when Trump and Sarah took a call from Scotland's then first minister, Alex Salmond. They'd been cordial and respectful to one another for many years. Trump, as an investor in the country, could not, however, fathom why Scotland's leading political minds were sacrificing one of the country's greatest assets with the proliferation of wind turbines. Or, as Trump insisted on calling them, "windmills"— a classic Trumpism, as Sarah put it. They are, of course, turbines, but Trump was deliberate in his language. Sarah raised her brows—he wanted to reinforce how archaic and out of date he believed this energy technology to be. Besides, as ever, the ordinary man on the street knew exactly what he meant.

The debate was hot, and Trump felt his voice was speaking for millions of ordinary citizens worried about the value of their homes with the influx of the massive wind structures being erected across the country. They appeared all over Scotland, sparking extensive debate and anger. Mountains and glens alike were deemed suitable for more and more turbines and the pylons needed to support them. Despite the challenges they already faced, Trump couldn't let the issue lie. Sarah was blunt in her assessment: "This wasn't just about the stupidity of erecting these monstrosities outside his property. It was the insanity of trading the country's greatest natural asset in exchange for gargantuan foreign tin structures. The country was being duped."

Salmond called, and Sarah passed her cell phone to Trump, who was sitting up front. Past the conviviality, Trump told him straight: "I like you Alex, but you are making a big mistake, and I will fight you on this." Sarah remembered the conversation well. Alex, in turn, said he'd enjoy the attention brought about by a public disagreement with Trump, claiming it would be good for him and his government.

Trump's response was plain: "Alex, if you fight with me, be warned, I hit below the belt."

That is typical Trump, for Sarah: in battle, he doesn't play fair, he plays to win, and he's honest about that. According to Sarah, there are no hidden agendas with Trump. You will know if you are friend or foe—you always know where you stand. In this case, it was arguably in Trump's interests to stay out of the battle. It would cost his business a great deal of money and disruption. Sarah reflected on the idiocy of the policy that Trump decided to challenge whatever the cost. He just couldn't let it go. "There was a bigger principle at stake that was worth the fight. Trump exposed the failings of the government's flawed energy agenda by directly calling out the issue from behind what they saw as the fog of spin and propaganda."

The turbines continued their march across Scotland. However, oil prices crashed shortly after that, and Salmond was forced to resign after he failed to win the confidence of the Scottish people in a vote over independence.

That's what sums DJT up to this EVP: "Trump is a fighter. He's not afraid to take blows. Attack is the best form of defense, in his view. Equally, he knows there are battles not worth the fight if you want to win the war."

CHAPTER 19

Sexism, Deals, and Learning to Believe

It was after midnight, and Sarah was dozing off. Don Jr. and I called. It was seven p.m. in New York City, and Trump was on the cusp of declaring all-out war on a past acquaintance and fellow New Yorker who'd thrown him insults on the eve of a high-profile golf tournament. This was not a time to be hurling fireballs at one man who could wipe out friends and allies alike.

"Malone, you try speaking to him!" the voices came simultaneously down the line.

Sarah was still relatively new in the job, and Don and I

had been putting her through her paces; testing her mettle, as she put it. Trump had put her in post, but she was still an unknown to the guys. She cast her mind back: "It's not easy forming relationships with the vast expanse of the Atlantic Ocean between you. I had to learn fast how to read the tone and inflection of my colleagues' voices, to understand the mood and atmosphere of head office."

The tension coming down the line that night instantly snapped her out of her slumber.

To the team, the cocky "past acquaintance" had made the ill-fated decision to mock Trump in the press earlier that day, and Donald was ready to let rip. The problem was, a retaliation at this time would alienate half their industry friends, Sarah explained. She had met this "past acquaintance" several months earlier when she'd hosted him for lunch at the Scottish property.

"I couldn't care less about gender and have a thick skin, but I'm no fool," Sarah said. "I know a chauvinist when I meet one."

It didn't go unnoticed that the man in question could not look her in the eye. "He wouldn't even look in my direction, let alone converse," she remembered. During the entire lunch, he directed his questions to her male colleague and then proceeded to thank him for his gracious hospitality before leaving without so much as a "pleased to meet you." Sarah laughs at it now—more a reflection of his insecurities than her gender—but at the time it irked her.

"I know I work in a male-dominated sector, but this man was an ignorant buffoon—I'd seldom encountered more misogynistic behavior. It's ironic that Trump gets labeled with this sort of tag when he's anything but. He had no issue appointing a woman in the top job to represent his interests in Scotland, even if this businessman wasn't prepared to acknowledge a female in the role. You could say, I'd have liked to give this chump a piece of my mind . . ." Her voice tailed off. She is very vocal about Trump's support for women and how he has no qualms about promoting strong women into his leadership team throughout his empire, and many of them stay with him for decades.

Sarah's thoughts darted back to that phone call, and she remembered how Don handed the phone to his father. Trump's voice was low and sullen: "Hello . . . Have you read what that so-and-so has said?"

The former acquaintance had attempted to belittle Trump while pumping himself up to the press. From Sarah's standpoint, Trump was entitled to lash out. Frankly, she'd have relished the opportunity, too, given how the man in question had treated her. However, there was more at stake than reacting to one person trying to take on Trump. She was sure this guy was heading for disaster—he would hoist himself by his own petard sooner or later. Her advice was to let him have his moment in the sun, to wait and see what the coming weeks would bring. Trump was unimpressed with her argument and curt to say the least.

"Getting Donald to back off is no easy feat. He listens but you darn well better know what you're doing, as he sharply reminded me that night: 'I'm holding you to account for this one, Sarah Malone. You'd better be right!'" She knows with the benefit of hindsight that she was to be proved right, but it might not have ended up that way.

The events of the next few days were almost biblical, Sarah recalled. You couldn't have made it up. Torrential rains and unprecedented winds swept across Scotland. Trump's golf course weathered the elements like a veteran soldier while their former friend's tournament was literally a washout, with part of its site falling apart and being washed away. To the team, Trump was vindicated, and it was the last time they ever spoke about the former friend who thought he could muscle up to Trump.

Sarah's seniority and position as a woman in the company have never been up for discussion. She's been afforded the same place at the table and has taken the heat and rolled with the punches like her male counterparts. Sarah sees it very clearly and simply: "Trump is a very progressive employer. He's not interested in gender; he's just interested in results."

Over the years, invariably, many men have attempted to patronize or circumvent her, even if they never get the chance to do it a second time, but she has never experienced this behavior with Trump. "He has always shown me the utmost respect, and despite his global success he never made me feel anything less than an equal. I find the offensive slurs leveled at him about his view of women upsetting. My experience is the complete opposite; he is seriously prowomen. There is no glass ceiling for my gender in The Trump Organization. I recall Trump once said, 'A tough woman in business is worth ten men.'"

The enormity of the issues Sarah has dealt with under Trump takes some beating. From fighting government leaders to conducting court cases, litigation, and global press conferences, and to making deals, hiring contractors, and setting up an entire operational team, she's had the lot. But that's not all. To Sarah, Trump is an enigma: you think you've figured him out and you might just be able to meet his demands, and then he'll blindside you. He misses nothing.

She recalls inspecting almost every inch of the property in Scotland some years back, in anticipation of Trump's arrival. All hands were on deck to preen, titivate, and polish. The expansive estate was in tip-top condition—at least she thought so.

DJT checked into his room. He'd been on site less than one hour, and she was called to his guest room. He beckoned her into his en suite. Visibly annoyed, he pointed to half an inch of chipped paintwork on the window ledge. "Sarah Malone, you have a bad person working here." One of the gardeners had knocked the painted ledge earlier that morning while watering the terrace plants.

Several hours later over lunch, Trump raised the small chip once again. It was playing on his mind. Considering she had 1,400 acres of land to manage, including 500 acres of world-class golf course to maintain, this chipped bit of paint was the least of her worries.

"How are you going to fix it?"

"The maintenance manager will get on to it, Mr. Trump."

"It will never look as good again, you know," he bellowed. She tried to reassure him that they'd fix it as good as new, but he groaned, and to her astonishment, he commanded that she get him the "stuff" and he'd fix it himself.

"There comes a point with Trump that the best response

is to act and not argue. I duly instructed my team to drop off the necessary tools in his room so he could touch up the offending chip of paint himself. He's the boss," she said.

Much later that day, she recalled being summoned by Keith Schiller, who was wide eyed as he ushered her into Trump's bathroom. Trump was now standing on a drop cloth, in his socks, tieless, his shirt tousled. Pointing at a two-liter can of paint by his feet, he lectured her on the volume of paint they were allegedly wasting. Proceeding to stick his finger into the adjacent pot of wood filler, he began to smear putty over the window ledge, barking, "I'm a really busy man, Sarah Malone, a really busy man, but nobody does this better than me!"

Sarah reflected on that extraordinary sight. "Trump possibly didn't see the funny side of it at the time, but it was highly amusing. And the truth is, he fixed that window himself that day, and he never raised the subject again."

While amusing, it raises a serious point for Sarah: the man gets things done and will be as prepared to do it himself as anyone. "He is a perfectionist, and he knows what he wants. When he sets his mind on something, there is no stopping him. But it's not always about instant gratification. He's also prepared to wait. On bigger-picture matters, he takes the long view."

She remembered back to 2010, when they were in the thick of construction. Sarah had hotfooted it over to Ireland to see what her Irish cousins had built in recent years. She was welcomed with open arms across the Emerald Isle and hopped over to Northern Ireland, too, but she was hooked on what she saw at Doonbeg in County Clare along the spectacular southwest coast of Ireland. This place had Trump written all over it. The dramatic coastal location and the quality of the property took Sarah's breath away. As if by telepathy, Trump called her as she departed the grounds of the Doonbeg estate. "Where are you, Sarah Malone?"

"Ireland, boss, at an incredible property overlooking the Irish Sea—you would love it."

With unbridled enthusiasm, Sarah described the idyllic sanctuary hugging the dramatic Irish coastline. "Is it for sale?" Trump jumped in.

Doonbeg was one of the hottest properties in Ireland, and she definitely wasn't getting for-sale signals. "No, boss, there are countless other venues on the market, but these guys have no interest in selling."

"Everything is for sale, Sarah Malone!" Trump was undeterred. The owners had thrown the kitchen sink at this site. No expense had been spared. Don Jr. and I flew over the following week and were equally impressed. Trump was insistent that she ask for their architectural layout and plans.

Sarah told her boss that it was an American-owned property and they were not going to hand over their drawings— and certainly not to Trump. He was not for backing off.

Sarah knows Trump, and he often asks for the impossible. She'd become accustomed to this sort of instruction. Even her best Scottish charm was not going to extract the plans from the general manager, Joe Russell, who thought she was having a laugh. The property was well and truly on Trump's radar. He would bide his time.

Four years later, with the challenges in the Irish economy taking their toll, the word was out that Doonbeg was on the market. Within less than six days, arguably one of the fastest transactions for an asset of this scale, Trump had snapped up Ireland's jewel in the crown for an incredible price.

"The ultimate dealmaker had struck again." Sarah chuckled. "His real estate footprint across the globe continued to expand rapidly over the years, but his multidimensional, indefatigable appetite for more always left me thinking he hadn't quite reached his pinnacle."

In 2012, Sarah was in Chicago and heading to Medinah for the Ryder Cup as a guest of the PGA. The tickets were red hot, and Trump decided to meet her there with Melania. It was an intense game. The US team was thrashing Europe until the final hour, and Trump was ebullient and full of fun. The atmosphere was electrifying. Trump, in his inimitable way, gestured to Keith, who was never far from reach, and a charming American host driving a golf cart appeared from nowhere. They were all invited to take a seat. Sarah was hesitant, her mind darting around. This cart was inside the ropes, and while they were VIP guests, they weren't officials and certainly not allowed behind the ropes.

The charming golf cart driver smiled widely. "Get in, get in," he urged. Trump, Melania, and Sarah climbed into the cart.

"I don't mind challenging the rules or even breaking them occasionally, but this was the Ryder Cup, and the rules were the rules—I didn't want to invite trouble," Sarah said.

The driver chatted feverishly to Trump, evidently an *Apprentice* fan thrilled to be seated next to one of America's greatest TV stars. They were whisked at speed along the course inside the boundary of cheering spectators.

"Go Trump! Trump! Trump! Trump for president!" The yelling was relentless from the sidelines, Sarah recalled.

Thumbs-ups, waving, hand slapping, and cheers of support reverberated as they whirled across the course. The support and adoration from the US people increased the farther they drove. The patriotism reached its climax that day as they all stood in the stand at the NBC tent. With Trump at the center, an almighty "USA! USA! USA!" erupted from the elated fans. Trump was in the thick of it. "The admiration and respect for him that day was never more evident as the packed grandstand of Americans clutched and high-fived The Donald," Sarah said as she smiles at the memory.

At home and abroad, Sarah has seen Trump avail himself to young and old, rich and poor. In her mind, he is magnetizing and not selective of whom he engages with. All men and women are equal. Everyone has an opinion of Trump, of course, formed mainly by what he or she thinks of him. For Sarah, the truth is somewhat different: for those who have met him, they like him, and many love him, whether they agree with his politics or not.

Sarah remembered the spring of 2016 when she was in New York attending a global Trump conference at one of the properties. In between sessions, she darted uptown for a quick one-to-one with the boss. The presidential race was in full flight, and access to the man himself was becoming increasingly difficult. Wading through the swaths of passing spectators, armed police patrolling the front of Trump Tower, and Secret Service agents frisking people at every turn, she finally reached the head office.

Trump appeared pleased to see her. The office was notably

calm. For a man who had been on the road for months, he looked remarkably fresh, she recalled. They chatted between interruptions: "Sarah Malone, I need to leave, but let's keep talking in the car." Trump was heading to the conference she was attending to give a brief address before resuming the presidential campaign. "She's coming with me," he hollered.

She was whisked away by one of the countless black-suited Secret Service officers with wires tucked behind their ears. Then she found herself on Fifty-Sixth Street, which was blockaded at both ends. Metal railings and flocks of NYPD officers manned the barricades as crowds began to amass, with everyone jockeying for position.

"This was insane. Trump can gather an audience, but this was in another league," Sarah said as she stood and headed back to the chair behind her desk.

Before her were five black armored vehicles, and she was bundled into the central car by the Secret Service. If it hadn't fully hit her before, she was now profoundly conscious that life, as she'd known it in Trump world, had changed. Cell phones aloft, the gathered masses erupted with shrieks and screams of excitement as Trump emerged from Trump Tower.

"Can you believe this, Sarah Malone?" He smiled as he stepped into the car.

"I felt less like a senior executive and more like an extra in a Hollywood movie," Sarah recalled. "I'd seen unprecedented attendance at press conferences and adoring fans grappling for his autograph or a picture in the past, but this was something else."

As they drove down Fifth Avenue, sirens blaring, Keith

rolled down the window of the car. Two young women were frantically chasing their cell phones at the bottom of their handbags as the vehicle sat stationary by traffic lights. Hyperventilating and falling to their knees, they screamed uncontrollably as Trump gave them a smile and waved directly back at them.

As they chatted in those moments, Sarah felt like she was having an out-of-body experience. She could barely focus on what Trump was saying. "I've traveled with Trump many times, I've even driven him myself on umpteen occasions, but I felt in my bones something was different. I knew at that moment, long before polling day, that I was sitting next to the future president of the United States of America."

If there is one thing Sarah has learned working with this man, it is not to underestimate him. Every time something happened in the campaign and everyone declared it was over and he'd blown it, he went forward and gained more ground. "That's the Trump I've seen in action for the past decade."

The forty-five-minute cab ride she'd taken earlier in the day to Trump Tower took a little over ten minutes as the police convoy whistled through the streets of New York and returned her to her destination. She rejoined the conference and Trump gave what she described as an exhilarating speech before jetting off to Mexico to resume his mission.

The events that followed changed the face of politics forever, and on inauguration day in Washington, DC, Sarah Malone sat close to the podium alongside hundreds of thousands of US citizens who had gathered to witness Trump being sworn in. He had defied all odds.

Sarah is effusive and deliberately protective of her boss—
because of who he is and what he's done for her, and what
she believes he has done for people wherever his projects sit.

"Trump has taught me a great deal, a lifetime of lessons,
but above all, he has proved over and over that anything is
possible if you believe."

CHAPTER 20

Sometimes the Deal
Comes Second

I can speak with authority about business sacrifice. For decades, The Trump Organization was driven and led by one man. Very rarely do corporations of this magnitude look to one individual over the course of fifty years for their focus, their strategy, and their energy. However, that is precisely what we did at the Trump Org. He was in charge for over four decades, shaping and building it with single-handed determination and vision. Now we have lost him.

As an organization, we have temporarily—maybe even permanently—lost our leader.

For many public organizations, the removal or displace-
ment of the CEO would probably be very different. It might
lead to temporary shock and loss of corporate value as Wall
Street reevaluated its share price following the removal of the
captain of the ship. Alternatively, if it happened in a private
operation like ours, it might mean people would temporarily
shuffle in their seats as they waited to see who took over and
on what course he or she was likely to steer the ship. However, The Trump Organization is different.

It was so centered on him, his achievements, his personality, his aura, his fame, that it *was* Donald J. Trump. Although
many great people made it work, the heartbeat of the company was driven by that one great man; his personality and
the essence of the company were intermingled into the very
fabric of the building and its operations, and so it was impossible to separate them.

His departure was not only a body blow to all of us who
had taken direction from him, some for over three decades,
but it also meant there was going to have to be a fundamental realignment of the business strategy and day-to-day
operations.

Those first few days after his victory at the polls were
strange. There was a sense of euphoria at his incredible
achievement—and many of us had played a role in that, no
matter how small—and a phenomenal high at the prospect of
DJT taking his business style into the most critical job in the
world. However, there was also a sense of unease about how
things might pan out internally. Where would we go from
here? How would the company operate? What was the strat-

egy going to be, and, most important, how could we work under the strictures imposed by the US Constitution and its political system?

From a practical perspective—and it's publicly documented, so I'm not revealing anything here—Trump removed himself from the day-to-day operations legally by creating trusts and naming his children and longtime CFO Allen Weisselberg as trustees.

We lost our leader, mentor, and the glue that held everything together, the guy who pushed the company forward and at the same time backed us up. There was never any better firepower than that! His absence had a profound effect on the business. Although everyone has tremendous respect and affection toward Don Jr. and Eric, who are extremely competent in their own rights, neither of them—nor anyone else, for that matter—is their father, and they would be the first to admit that.

Even the practical implications of the postinaugural legal ramifications were onerous and incredibly restrictive. Before implementing many decisions, the company now has to go through two layers of outside, independent, third-party review—an ethics adviser and business adviser. Each of those is a well-known international law firm that essentially vets all material transactions and issues full-blown legal opinions that govern what the business can and can't do. Imagine trying to run a business with that kind of stricture around your neck! It hardly makes for swift and agile decision making. That happens day in and day out for almost every big decision it has to make.

We also voluntarily agreed not to pursue new business transactions outside the United States. Considering that a significant part of our future business plan was based on international expansion, this restriction significantly curtailed our ability to function as a healthy business. Many commentators—and probably critics, too—would say that this tying up of the business so that it can't expand in the way it had planned is right. Why should the company develop for the benefit of DJT while he's in the most powerful position on the planet?

However, we're talking about a business that supports not just the Trump family but also thousands of people and their families across the globe. So DJT's sacrifice, while utterly personal, of course, went well beyond him and affected so many others. I know he's conscious of that and it also weighs heavily on his mind.

The business will survive and continue to progress, but his presidency affects everyone, from the greenkeeper to the waitress to the bellboy. Those who say he ran for president for the money are so wide of the mark it's just laughable. This is a guy who put the very future of his business on the line, knowing that it would be tied up in red tape for years while he was away trying to sort out our great nation's problems.

If his only concern was making more and more money, he'd have sat tight, continued doing what he was doing, and watched his wealth grow. Instead, he saw the challenges facing the American people and our economy and decided to invest tens of millions of his own money to make a change. As someone who knows his business inside and out, I can say very few wealthy Americans would be willing to take the extreme financial hit he signed on for.

The protests and the day-to-day hammering in the news had an impact on all of us, too, but probably not in the way that people expect. The result is that it brought the team together and it's just another challenge that we all faced. Wherever you go in the Trump empire, every single member of his staff is proud of the decision he's taken and fully supports him in that endeavor.

What is the cost of lost opportunities? On a daily basis, many people in the organization have lots of unique potential projects coming across their desks that they couldn't touch. Where's the value in that? The protesters and malcontents who have gone out of their way to try to destroy the businesses, by blocking phone lines and making fake bookings only then to pull them, are a pain in the ass, but they won't divert the team from the cause.

In actuality, they have brought the team closer together. Staff gets harassed and abused, but we all know that the man is doing it for the greater good. Most sigh and shake it off, but it can get a little wearing and tiresome.

A ten-year-old coming home upset that he's been bullied at school because a parent works for the Trump Org is pretty low. I know of one member of the team whose young child— just a year old—was subject to really offensive abuse online, including being called a bastard, because the mother works for the organization. Whatever you think of the president and his policies, what kind of cruel savage would target abuse at a young child like that? These keyboard warriors— anonymous, of course—are cowards and scumbags.

Beyond that there are the physical threats—staff have been spat on and attacked—so we all have to be careful and take the necessary precautions. I never leave my home without my trusted Glock, and I'm not the only one in the company who considered a firearm to be an absolute necessity. Thank God for the Second Amendment.

I spent a tremendous amount of time responding to the ridiculous demands of partisan members of Congress who seemed to have nothing better to do than harass The Trump Organization. I received lots of inquiries from certain individual members of Congress who seemed to revel in trying to find fault, trip us up, or criticize us. It's so apparent that they are attacking the company—they are abusing their position in government to attack a private company with an endgame of trying to weaken the president—but it won't work. We were smarter, better organized, and more nimble than any of them could ever be, as well as having right on our side.

Every week, I received letters from members of the House or Senate that contained pages and pages of subpoena-like demands that no other private-sector company was forced to deal with. We understood that it's a unique circumstance and accepted the scrutiny that came with it, but there's a fine line between legitimate inquiry and outright harassment. These bloated congressional committees, some of which have hundreds of people on staff, are using public resources to launch politically motivated attacks to try to trash a private company that thousands of families rely on for their living, often for reasons based only on conjecture. Many of these letters use as their only source media accusations without ever referencing any facts—and we all know that most of these claims are fake news and spurious in the extreme.

It's incredible that a member of Congress would cite an unsubstantiated news report that references an anonymous informant and then rely on that shaky information (which would never pass muster in a real court of law) as the basis of an attack on us. This is not something that happened once; it was repeated over and over and over again.

Our opponents' tactic was transparent: to bombard us with nonsense so we couldn't perform our essential day-to-day responsibilities. Guess what? It didn't work. I'm not trying to single anyone out, but take a look at Congressman Elijah Cummings's masterpieces. They're public documents and available online. To be clear, I have a great deal of respect for him and admire his many achievements, but let's be honest, his district is plagued with problems, and he should spend more time addressing the needs of the decent people who live there instead of wasting his time harassing the company to burnish his political image, which is clearly meant to disrupt the Trump administration.

ISIS has been all but destroyed, the economy is booming, unemployment has been the lowest it's been in forty-nine years, and the Supreme Court—with two Trump appointees—is finally heading in the right direction. If you see the profound harm the presidency has caused Trump's personal wealth, and how little it matters when he's succeeding in the White House, the narrative in Congress makes you feel like you are taking crazy pills.

I admit I wasn't happy when Obama was elected. He

hadn't achieved much in the real world, and I could never understand the credentials of a "community organizer." It was clear that he was an articulate, well-educated, well-mannered guy, but he didn't have the qualifications to run the US economy, especially in a time of crisis. However, I woke up the next morning and said to myself that I'd support him because he was our president. His success would mean that the country would succeed, and I genuinely wished him well. I don't understand how others reject this type of thinking.

The United States is a democracy, and respecting that system—while it's not perfect—benefits everyone. It works better than the majority of governments in the civilized and not-so-civilized worlds, and we should accept the decisions of the majority.

The president himself is aware of the sacrifices his staff has had to make to ensure that his administration succeeds. When Damian and I were having dinner with him in the White House, the president revealed that he felt he had the weight of the world on his back, but that it was a load worth carrying. "I do miss it," President Trump said about his previous life in the organization, but added, "It's a price worth paying. I thought that I could do a good job because this country had been heading down the wrong path. You see what's happening in California? People are beginning to worry about their safety. They want to be safe."

We chatted about my own recent personal experiences in San Francisco, where you can't walk a block without being accosted by vagrants. "San Francisco used to be such a beautiful city," the president said, "and we need to return it to the people the way it used to be so that the people feel safe."

The president's sacrifice is only likely to continue. At that same dinner, in the magnificent and humbling surroundings of the Blue Room, he revealed that he was prepared to go through it all again. As we asked him whether he was likely to run for president again, he paused for a moment and looked at the portraits of the presidents around him and quietly said, "Yes, it's something I'm already looking forward to. We're doing a great job and are ahead of schedule, but we've still so much more to achieve."

It's clear that President Trump feels a great weight of public service and clear that he is the right man to turn our country around. This is not about the money—quite the opposite. So far, The Trump Organization has suffered financially, and so has he. He doesn't take a salary, and he knows that this could be costing him hundreds of millions of dollars in the long run, but he is determined to see the project through.

I remember when there was a tremendous uproar about the proposed construction of a mosque near Ground Zero. It's clear that a city of New York's scale and cultural mix needs mosques as much as it needs churches and synagogues, but the sensitivities around that area should be obvious to any reasonable person. DJT stepped in to try to buy the site and offered to locate the mosque in a more appropriate area. That wasn't a deal aimed at doing anything other than diffusing an issue that was tearing the city apart and creating a toxic environment emotionally, socially, and culturally. It was stirring up hatred. He was trying to step in and calm everyone down and achieve a reasonable resolution that suited all parties. However, he was battered and attacked for even trying to help out, as "experts" (yup, them again) tried to make it look like he wanted to benefit from the deal financially. That was so far wide of the mark that it was laughable, but it made for a great story, so the media saw it as an opportunity to take a cheap shot at him. Again.

Look, there are many examples in history that teach us that self-sacrifice can often lead to benefits for the greater good. Despite the day-to-day rough-and-tumble of our reality, we all hope Trump continues for a second term, because it's a dangerous world we live in, and the America First attitude is a refreshing departure from prior paths.

We know the world is getting smaller, and to some extent, we now live in a global village. However, the United States continues to subsidize countries around the world on the basis of treaties and deals that, in some cases, date back to the troubling days and years after World War II. Time has moved on, and yet we're still being looked at as the world's banker. It has to stop.

As the president himself told us as we stood in Lincoln's bedroom in the White House admiring the original copy of the Gettysburg Address, when Lincoln initially gave that speech he was heavily criticized and torn to shreds by the media and so-called establishment for a poor address that was weak, incoherent, and lacking drive. On November 24, 1863, the *Harrisburg Patriot & Union* produced a lengthy and brutal editorial in which it stuck the boot into Lincoln's speech. It called the address "the silly remarks of the president" and added, "For the credit of the nation we are willing that the veil of oblivion shall be dropped over them and that they shall be no more repeated or thought of."

Just think of that!

Nothing changes among the media, and they still think they know best, despite, in the main, having no expertise of their own other than to criticize others' efforts. There isn't an American schoolkid now who doesn't know the opening lines: "Four score and seven years ago . . . ," and history now considers it to be one of the greatest political speeches ever made.

I'm sure that history, uncorrupted by the nasty political spin, will illuminate the great work Trump has achieved on behalf of the American people. He will emerge as one of the greatest presidents of modern times. Believe me.

CHAPTER 21

Man of the People

Wherever you go in The Trump Organization—and in the more practical and less political areas of the White House—you will find people who don't have a bad word to say about President Trump. During my trips inside 1600 Pennsylvania Avenue, I consistently come across people, from waitstaff to secretaries, military personnel to cleaners, who don't have anything other than praise for the kindness shown by and politeness of the president.

As I've said before, sure, Trump can explode like Krakatoa when he needs to, but the nature of the man is so different from what the critics and journalists—and even some authors—would have you believe. He utterly believes in seeing through what he's promised to, whenever possible, and he hates letting anyone down if he can avoid it.

He always has time for people, wherever and whenever he is. I've seen him sitting down for dinner in restaurants or having a private planning meeting, and people will come up and interrupt him, and he still will stop what he's doing—even if he's midfork—and let them take a selfie, have a quiet word, or get an autograph. I'm not so sure I'd be so graceful and forgiving if someone approached me as I was dining with my wife or colleagues and stepped straight in to take a picture.

However, he never bats an eyelid or pauses for a heartbeat. He knows such things come with the territory. He doesn't just do it quickly and brush people off, either; he wants to stop, chat, and ask people how their day is going, what they are eating, or what they think of that particular, restaurant, club, gig, or whatever. He is so polished and effortless at it. DJT is a very gregarious person; he loves being among people, enjoys listening to their stories and hearing what they're up to, and he's fascinated by the views of the people he comes across on everything from the prison population to the decor of the place he might be visiting.

Even now, as president of the United States, he still wants to stop and chat with people about how things are going and what they're thinking—if such people can penetrate the ring of steel. It's not something he particularly enjoys, having that kind of protection from the wider public, but he knows it's necessary to ensure his safety and to keep the office of president safe. The special agents in the Secret Service know he is one of theirs, and he respects the office and their job, and that of all our police and military personnel. After being shunned and treated with disdain for years, he has brought back a clear sense of pride, from the very top, for the job that all our law enforcement personnel do for the nation.

Have you seen some of the events he has held for the navy, the army, and the air force? They are packed solid with military personnel and their families, and his support for them is clear and unequivocal.

There was an evening we were planning an event at Trump World Tower at a time when I was president of the board. When units would come up for sale we had a broker permanently on site to discreetly and efficiently handle all the resales that might occur in the building. Remember, there were 360-plus units in this magnificent building, and there was always demand from people wanting to get access to it.

Because of the nature of the clients in the building, we'd tend to have one person handle all the details, because we're not talking about you or me here, we're talking about Hollywood movie stars, top-end sports stars, and politicians who wanted everything to be handled efficiently and discreetly. They had enough shit to deal with without having to go backward and forward to real estate agents, removal companies, lawyers, and the like. For a long time, we had a fabulous broker in Michelle, and this particular evening was to be her introduction to the people at TWT who might need her services in the future.

DJT was always keen to attend these events, to make sure that he was on hand in case any queries cropped up, and just as president and chairman of the company, to make sure things all went smoothly—it was his name on the building, after all.

So, there was a cocktail reception that had been meticulously planned and prepared for to begin at six p.m. and end at eight. All the residents of the building would have the chance to meet Michelle and learn who she was and where she would be should they ever need her. It was just another day at the office, and these kinds of events were pretty standard for Mr. Trump, so he and I, along with his bodyguard, the great Keith Schiller, hopped in a limo and headed out into the NYC traffic and on toward our destination: my home.

Now, anyone who has ever been to New York knows that the traffic can be chaotic and slightly frenetic, but we were expecting to be traveling for only a few minutes to TWT. I remember that we were chatting away about the day we'd just had and discussing some details of a particular project when we approached a red light on Second Avenue and Fifty-Fourth or Fifty-Fifth.

A taxicab came hurtling up behind us and rear-ended us way down the street. All of us were sent flying from our seats.

The noise and impact were tremendous, and the beautiful limo was pretty severely damaged. It was a hell of a scare for all of us, but thankfully, none of us was injured other than a few bumps and bruises. I was completely stunned and didn't quite know what to do next. Keith, of course, went into preservation mode and was determined to make sure the boss was well looked after. However, Mr. Trump was cool personified. He knew it would take a while to sort things out, and while we were all a bit shaken up, he dusted himself down and stepped out of the car to take a look.

DJT's first thought was to make sure we were okay, but he had other people to think about, too. Despite Keith's protestations, DJT decided that we had to press on; otherwise, we'd be late—and he didn't want to let down Michelle or the residents of his building.

Keith, himself ex–US Navy and a former NYPD cop, remembered it well: "It was one hell of a crash. It wasn't so much the damage to us or the car, but it gave us all a bit of a jolt. I remember the boss wanted me to stay behind and handle things, and he said, 'George and I will just walk over there.'

"'Walk over there'? It was my job to keep him safe from any crazy people or worse, who might want to take a potshot at him, and here I was, standing there swapping insurance details as he walked away with George toward his event. I wasn't happy about it, but what can you do? If the boss says do something, you do it. He didn't worry about his safety; he wanted everyone in that building to be happy, and he had a job to do. No matter how many times I advised him not to take these risks, he did it time and time again. Whether we were at a hearing, on the campaign trail, and when he was the boss of Trump Org, he just never wanted to let anyone down."

I remember it like that, too. He said, "Come on, George, let's walk. Keith can figure this out; we need to get to the event."

From DJT's perspective, he had a commitment, and he didn't want to keep people waiting. What's a little car accident and a long walk when you have his sense of obligation—not wanting to keep people waiting?

He often does the kind of thing that exposes him to unnecessary risk out of a sense of obligation to the people in his buildings and the members of his clubs. He didn't want to miss Michelle meeting people. Yes, it was in his business interests, but the reality is he didn't have to do that. He'd had an accident, and he could always have missed a meeting—people often do. Who would walk out of a car wreck and worry about a scheduled meeting? I doubt it'd be at the forefront of anyone else's mind. Punctuality is important to him because there are so many meetings he has to attend and he hates to keep people waiting, and he hates being kept waiting by others, so he's all too aware of how irritating it would be if he did it.

Once when he met Peter Dawson, the head of the Royal and Ancient Golf Club of St Andrews in Scotland (the home of golf), we were running late from our overnight flight to Scotland. Trump didn't stop to get changed once we touched down, or to have a drink or anything like that; he wanted to dash to get there. Sometimes you're late and can't help it, that's life, but Trump doesn't like to keep people waiting. Many others nowadays don't seem to care about missing meetings or being late. That sense of responsibility, civility, and politeness has been lost in many people's lives.

However, he didn't want to keep people waiting and delay Michelle, and so we hopped up the steps and wandered into the event, and he even gave a little speech to make everyone laugh and feel relaxed. This time it was my turn to squirm. He told everyone in the building—my neighbors and friends—a story about how a young lady was working for him as one of his fantastic executive assistants and how I'd come along and stolen her from him. She is, of course, now my wife.

CHAPTER 22

Father and Boss

E ric Trump's office reflects the same taste as his father's office, but it is less cluttered and not nearly as eclectic. And not quite as big. Eric's desk faces out onto the main thoroughfare of the operation that handles the Trump family's golf complexes and hotel assets. To his left is Ivanka's office. A short hop to the right is Don Jr.'s.

One floor above, his father's office is now locked and clear of all the memorabilia collected over fifty years in an astonishing business career, awaiting a decision as to what will make it to the presidential library when that day finally comes. Portraits, framed magazine covers, essential memorabilia, all lie stacked, numbered, and cataloged in the corridor outside his office, awaiting their place in history. The silence in that guarded corridor—where formerly there was endless hustle and bustle—is eerie. Secret Service agents pervade the building; one stands guard not far from that once vibrant office. No one enters or leaves without a search, a scan, and an appointment. Bomb-sniffing dogs abound; marksmen stand guard in the lobby.

After a string of executives from the company finally ended their requests for time, information, and answers, Eric began to reflect on the man who is his father, his onetime boss, and now the forty-fifth president of the United States of America.

As he leant back in his simple office chair contemplating the difficulties of running a complex business now hamstrung by his father's lofty position, his back was to the window with the Hudson River in the distance. There is a bundle of photographs—many with his father, most with his wife, Lara, and their young child, Luke—beaming down on him. An electronic picture frame beside his left arm flicks through a string of images of his young family, too. On a pinboard on the wall to the left above his head are a plethora of dollar bills, each signed by his father—GREAT GOING and WITH LOVE, DAD— recognition of previous bets that DJT had lost with his middle son. Eric chuckled as he remembered the handful of bets with which he has managed to secure a much-wanted victory against his ultracompetitive father.

On the opposite wall, framed newspaper articles and magazine covers proliferate, one particularly standing out: the copy of an article about Trump transferring the power of the empire to his children after winning the most prized contest on the planet. The thick Sharpie pen is unmistakable. KIDS, YOU'RE THE BEST IN THE WORLD! LOVE, DAD, it beams.

That is what Eric Trump reflects on most.

Eric looked into the sun, hopped up to crank up the air conditioning, and then reflected. "He's got an amazing gut instinct—when people swim downriver he's always swimming the other way. He has never followed the crowd." For Donald J. Trump, there is no question of just doing what others do or following the party line—he goes where his instincts tell him. That's what singles him out. That's what led him to 1600 Pennsylvania Avenue. "When there are two options on the table, he'll often find a third way that no one had thought of before—and you know what? He's almost always right."

For Eric, his brother, and his two sisters, growing up was not like it was for any other kid on the block (there is, of course, also a much younger brother, Barron). Sure, to them life was normal, but how simple could it have been? Their father was one of the most recognizable faces on the planet— not to mention the reams of newsprint and hours of airtime he dominated.

Eric remembers what Trump was like as a dad to a bunch of young, energetic kids who were clearly more vulnerable as a consequence of their dad's position than most. To us, it would have seemed surreal, but to Eric, it was pretty straight-forward. "When we lived upstairs, he was on sixty-seven [the sixty-seventh floor of Trump Tower], and my siblings and I were on sixty-eight, and we had living rooms on sixty-six. In the mornings, just as we were heading off to school, I would head downstairs to say goodbye and he would kiss me and say, "Remember, no drinking, no drugs, and no smoking— and get good grades."

Eric was six years old and barely even capable of doing

basic math. He knows the quip was a joke that really wasn't aimed at their young minds quite yet, at least. "However, the message got through, and we knew what was expected of us. He never said it in a strict way, but rather in a loving, caring way like any other father. He always worried about us."

This was at a time when Donald J. Trump's business was under scrutiny and facing some significant, and well-documented, financial troubles. "He was going through hell at that point, but he was thinking of his kids, and it was very telling."

Trump always told them not to drink or do drugs. It's a message he has reiterated for decades. "This is a man who has never had a sip of alcohol in his life and yet people think he's compulsive. But he has led a very clean life, and that is what separates him from others—he is clean and focused, despite what is often said. He's never compulsive."

To the outside world, the life of the Trump siblings must have been gilded and comfortable, with them wanting for nothing. The high life—literally in Trump Tower—seems so alien to most people in the outside world. These kids never went to struggling schools or had to fight for financial support.

Trump didn't spend much time taking his kids to baseball practice or shuttling them to classes, but the kids did spend an incredible amount of time in their private classroom: the office of Donald J. Trump. "Most kids will resent that because they want their dad to take them to their practices, recitals, or competitions, but we knew he was out working, building casinos, developing other properties, and running a company," Eric said.

That was just normal life for the Trump children. They

didn't know anything different and learned a great deal from their father and that incredible work ethic. "He's still a workaholic to this day, of course, and so we spent more time in that work environment than anywhere else," Eric said. "It was just fabulous—and for us it was normal; we didn't know anything else. There was never, 'Let's go and spend three weeks on a boat in the Med,' as our friends would. That just wasn't our way of doing things; we didn't do vacations like other people. He was busting his chops, and he was ultimately working for us: to provide an education and a great life."

For the children, this is their rock: the need to work hard for what they get and the need to prove themselves at the very bottom of the ladder before they are given a chance to move into the higher echelons of the Trump Org hierarchy or to make any bold decisions without Dad by their side. Eric remembered lots of hard work on various sites, because their father wanted them to learn the value of money, of hard work, and of the skills required to make a success of business and life.

When they were barely in their teens, they were learning plastering, plumbing, carpentry, and other skills that would enable them to have the understanding of the trades required when entering the field of real estate development.

To Donald J. Trump it was utterly critical that his children have an excellent grounding in the very basics of development—and that meant working long hours on site for very little money, to understand the processes and the difficulties of achieving greatness. It's rare for a family business to be successful in the third generation, because that generation often develops more of an interest in vacations and sports cars than hard work. Even Hillary Clinton praised Trump for teaching his kids to love ambition.

When Eric was twelve, Trump bought Seven Springs, which had previously been owned by the Rockefeller family, the H. J. Heinz family, and the Meyer family, owners of the *Washington Post*. It's hundreds of acres in Bedford, New York—in one of the top five wealthiest zip codes in the United States—in a town where if you have four acres, it's a mansion. It has sixty rooms and thirteen bedrooms, and there were a bunch of other houses on the estate that were ripe for redevelopment.

"Not only did he want us to work, we really wanted to as well—and we initially started with the stonemasons and got stuck in with the construction crews and the like," Eric said. This was no smooth ride for the kids in their early teens; they weren't there to kill time until they got bored of the exciting stuff and then could spend daddy's money. This went on for years.

The message from DJT was clear: "He wasn't the micromanaging parent, he said go and spread your wings and learn."

Some of the learning may have made ordinary mom and pops wince, or at the very least step in and put a stop to it— but not DJT. "One summer, as a kid, twelve or thirteen years old, I was cutting rebar with an acetylene torch. . . ." Eric reminisced.

That wasn't all—Eric would often be seen on the family estates somewhere out and about cutting the grass, but not with your usual lawnmower. "I had a diesel tractor, and I was so light that the springs would almost throw me off the seat and so I had to buckle myself in." It was all about cultivating that necessary work ethic and giving Eric and his siblings the vision to see that nothing would be achieved without long hours at work.

For some of Eric's contemporaries, their spending was not on clothes or drink but more illicit and life-changing substances, demons that some are still fighting to this day. But not Eric and Co. "We were busting our asses, so we weren't doing the things our friends were doing and ending up in rehab and the like."

Eric stopped in his tracks and shuddered at the memory of those who went down the wrong path in life. He knows that the advice from DJT was another part of his father's grand plan to not only provide his kids with the best education, as he saw it, for life in the organization, but also to ensure the tentacles of drugs, drink, and other sinister enticements were kept well out of their way.

Even now, the skills that Eric learned as a teenager creep back up to the surface on a regular basis and get used to full effect. "It was raining a couple of weekends ago, I was antsy, and I realized there was no electrical outlets in our closet at home, so I thought I'd just go do it myself and get it done. So, there I was wiring up the closet, trying to get everything fixed, and Lara said, 'You're going to electrocute yourself!'"

He laughed out loud but also with a little incredulity that his wife doesn't believe he can get the screwdrivers out and fix things himself. Even his people ask him to come and help hang dry wall or pick up marble for their kitchen, because they know he can do it well or because they don't quite believe it and want to see the boss do some hard, physical work. When it's time to plant the proverbial ceremonial tree, the boys get down and dirty.

He doesn't use the gold spades, he gets out the backhoe.

Eric believes that Luke should follow in his own father's footsteps. "I hope my kid is going to be exactly the same; he'll be cutting grass the same way I did, doing the same things I did for those vital lessons that I learned. I can't think of a better way to bring up a child and instill in them the need for hard work and an understanding of the value of a dollar."

Does that cause any regret on the part of Trump's children? Do they feel stifled or even under pressure from their father? Certainly not in Eric's eyes. As far as he's concerned, he's merely an integral part of the team that has to answer to the boss like anyone else, whenever and wherever they are.

"People ask, 'Is he micro or macro?' I can't tell you how many times at six a.m. I got calls about the layout of a floor, where the toilets might be placed, or the construction of a bunker—no one could ever imagine the level of granularity he would focus on. He always had incredible attention to detail. Yet, at the same time he could be very macro. In time, he came to trust that we had his eye for detail and quality."

Eric will never forget when he first came into the company. Vegas was the first building site he was involved in—Eric built 90 percent of it, 1,282 rooms on the strip. He'd just started the project, and DJT was telling them to go figure out the building and sales, go figure out how to negotiate with the banks. Eric and Jason Greenblatt—a former EVP and general counsel at The Trump Organization, now assistant to the president and special representative for international negotiations—walked into the room with all the lenders, and all Eric heard ringing in his ears was, "Go negotiate a good, long deal."

Eric smiled to himself at the memory and the challenges,

but he knows that his dad always had his back, as he did with the rest of the team. It's a message from Trump that keeps emerging over and over again: "I'm here if you have a question but go figure it out for yourself." That's the DJT mantra—sink or swim. He is able to get the best out of people.

Eric is acutely aware that that support works from the bottom to the very top, and he knows how many people started at the base and worked their way up to the higher echelons of the organization: it's the Trump way. The Trump Org is full of people who believe in that mantra and have stuck with Eric's father through thick and thin. "He built a foundation of incredibly loyal people who have stuck with him, the family, and the company. We're a very close family. Look at some of the people here. Amanda Miller started as a server at Westchester, became our marketing intern, and years later is running marketing for the entire company. She is family to us; you don't hear about that in other organizations. It's the story that is *never* told about The Trump Org. People associate 'You're fired' with my father and the company through *The Apprentice*, but it's the exact opposite. Many people are here for life and are truly cherished members of our family. And Sarah Malone in Scotland is another—she, too, has become part of our family. There's too many of those examples for it to be just coincidence."

One of those guys given his chance—like so many others throughout the Trump Org—was Brian Baudreau. He's a street-smart guy from New York who became a driver for DJT and drove the Trump kids to school, looking after those most-prized Trump assets. While The Trump Organization was working on Trump International Las Vegas, someone was needed to ferry people to and from the site and to handle delivering essential documents. Brian put his hand up and volunteered.

Eric remembered that they needed someone to bring out the architects, and Brian volunteered again. "He was there all the time, with his hand up. He just always wanted to be involved and he did an unbelievable job. He went from driving my father and taking us to school when we were young to the general manager of a billion-dollar job on the Las Vegas strip—it was on time and on budget; others were delayed and over budget and turned into a nightmare.

"We were under budget, and it was a better project than anyone could imagine. We brought in a hotelier who was a bit stiff, and we soon realized he wasn't our type of guy, so who was in the background with his hand up? Brian. He said, 'How hard could it be?' Also, 'Give me a few weeks, I'll get up to speed,' and ten years later he's still the general manager doing an incredible job."

For Eric, that's what marks out The Trump Organization—and DJT in particular—as different and innovative. Put yourself out there, take on more challenging roles, get things done as agreed, on time and on budget, and you'll be a great success.

That's what Trump loves. "It's the loyalty shown to people who do a great job," Eric said.

Isn't that easy to say, when you're born with the Trump name and are inevitably going to be working your way to the top? Isn't it all a bit too easy, to be given the job on a plate? "Sure, it's nepotism," Eric said, "but no other person would have said to a twenty-year-old kid, 'Go build a billion-dollar project' like he did to me with Vegas. Sure, he was there to help, but no one likes to go to DJT with problems. You have to have solutions. It was incredible what he trusted us with. We had to bust our chops to achieve it, but it was amazing, and we got it done. We never let him down.

"Believe me, if we'd messed up, we wouldn't be here today."

That pathway, that apprenticeship, has led to the greatest challenge of all for Eric, Don, and Ivanka, and to the highest level of trust from their father to date for them and the rest of the team on the twenty-fifth and twenty-sixth floors of Trump Tower in New York City.

He did it in the most significant way possible when he signed over his entire life's work to take over the biggest job on the planet. Eric thinks this trust and confidence is incredible. The whole point of these stories about the people in the company is to show that it's not the people with pedigrees or MBAs who do the best—they're the people who last the shortest, according to Eric—or the person with the perfect résumé. It's the doers, the people always on site all the time, the hard workers, and people who can cut through nonsense and red tape. And Eric thinks his dad can read through BS pretty well, too. Three-quarters of the questions he asks people he already knows the answers to—you're not conning or fooling the guy.

DJT is a guy who came out of Brooklyn and Queens and had the vision—when other developers were doing mid-rise buildings in the neighborhood—to go into Manhattan and develop new buildings. Eric reflected on how he moved from there to Chicago and Vegas, Hawaii and Scotland, Fifth Avenue and Wall Street, and a plethora of other buildings and golf courses.

"We were building in Dubai, India, Ireland, and Turkey, to

name but a few. Our buildings, hotels, and golf courses were everywhere, and then all of a sudden *The Apprentice* became the number one TV show, and we had fifteen seasons of being a top-rated show. It was unheard of. I remember being in the office when NBC asked us all to sign for an additional two seasons. Despite the huge monetary value, he turned it down. It wasn't about the money; the country was in trouble and he wanted to fix it."

That, to Eric, is the mark of the man, the mark of his father, the man who always wants to stay one step ahead of the field. To push for more. He's not interested in the money or the fame, he has that already; he wants to do his bit and be the man who tries to fix things when he sees they're so obviously broken. The man who gives people what they want: to make America great again. The man who, when everyone else is swimming downstream, is heading past them upstream. Who else would have given it all up—the money, the fame, and the TV series—to stand against a string of honed, polished, and prepared politicians who had spent their whole lives preparing for the ultimate job on the planet?

"I laugh when people say my father is profiting off the presidency. He turned down hundreds of millions of dollars from *The Apprentice* alone to take the chance to run against seventeen of the toughest Republican candidates that were brought out to challenge for the nomination. Then there was Hillary Clinton and her dynasty who outraised us seven to one and had the mainstream media in her pocket. Yet, despite all the odds, he went on to become the forty-fifth president of the United States."

The man who swims upstream.

CHAPTER 23

My Father, Mr. President

Eric laughed as he revealed how DJT will sometimes call from Air Force One, and they'll chat and shoot the breeze. He is always reminded of the magnitude of the job when his dad comes on the line, because before he gets to speak to him, he hears, "Mr. Trump, this is the commander of Air Force One, and we have the president of the United States for you . . ." And he has that from the White House, too, when he hears them say, "Mr. Trump, this is the White House operator, the president of the United States is on the other line for you. . . ."

"I say, 'Hey, pops! I miss you.' I'm always reminded of the gravity of the position, though."

That determination to succeed continues in the White House today. Eric sees it each and every day, despite the constant criticism and battering his father takes from so many different angles, from so many different commentators and politicians. "They said the economy had no hope, and yet it's up thirty-five percent. They said ISIS couldn't be defeated; there's no way the caliphate can be smashed. However, it's gone from forty thousand people fighting for it to little more than a thousand. And then there's Kim Jong-un . . . every one of these guys who criticize him [Trump] can't even imagine achieving half of what he's done so far."

It's clear that Eric has the mainstream media in his sights here. He shook his head as he said, "These media guys are so dishonest. They claim he's achieved nothing, and look what he's done." He has in mind North Korea in particular. "You need someone to be a bully to defeat a bully. Someone who tiptoes around the problem won't work. Someone had to stand up to the bully to get in his face."

Eric and his siblings are most proud of the trust their father has placed in them to continue his work while he concentrates on making America great again. It's something Eric hopes he can share with his own children. However, he's also driven to prove people wrong—because there are many people out there desperate to see them fail. The fact that Trump hasn't placed the company—which sits in a special trust—in the hands of anyone else speaks volumes to Eric, and the family connection continues to make Eric smile. As a family unit, it transcends business and probably politics more. "Everything we've done over the past fifteen years we've done together.

When we did *The Apprentice* I was on for seven seasons, and Don and Ivanka were on for nine. We did it all together."

Was that the same when Trump decided to become president? Was it a family decision, a family affair? Absolutely. It was ultimately Trump's gut instinct that led him there, but it needed to be the whole team, the entire family, to buy into project White House. Eric remembered sitting in his office talking about the possibility, and DJT said, "Kids, let's do this!" That was just a couple of days before he went down the escalator and made the announcement in front of the world's cameras at Trump Tower.

The "Let's" referring to the family, not "I," was essential to DJT, his family, and the whole team, some of whom joined him on that brutal campaign trail. "It was 'Let's do this,' not 'I'll do it,'" Eric said. "I didn't know what the caucus process was; I didn't know the first thing about politics in those first few weeks.

Eric had to speak against seasoned Republicans and their campaign managers who were standing for the post, too; he had to speak in gymnasiums to convince people his father was their best choice as candidate against people like Ted Cruz, Marco Rubio, Jeb Bush, Mike Huckabee, and others, trying to connect and be comfortable. The odds were massively stacked against Trump and his team, but they lived in swing states for months and operated as a unit—and Eric thinks Trump's innate trust in them was critical.

DJT could have had a yacht in the Caribbean, or relaxed and played golf every day and had fun with his family. He had the jets and helicopters and properties, and lived an incredibly comfortable life. However, Eric said he put in nearly 100 million of his own money and faced seventeen seasoned politicians who had prepared for this for their whole lives. "There were sons of former presidents, people who had been born and raised in the shadow of Capitol Hill, they winded and dined the necessary people, and we had to go against these political animals—and we won! My father had balls of steel. He understood the voice of the American people. I mentioned swimming against the tide. When people told him to swim with the tide, he went the other way."

Eric thinks this was emphasized no better than during that very first serious TV debate among the candidates hoping to win the Republican ticket. More than twenty-four million tuned in—the most watched primary debate of all time. The debate was fierce, almost brutal, and no quarter was taken or given. The pressure was intense.

And yet there was a moment when it would have been comfortable for Trump to crumble, to follow the crowd, to be the real politician. However, that's not his way. "People were trying to bait him, and Bret Baier [the Fox News anchor] asked the candidates to raise their hand if they were not prepared to support whichever candidate came out as the victor."

Immediately DJT put his hand up, while no one else did. Bret started to ask why Trump wouldn't pledge his allegiance to the Republican Party and his support to the successful candidate. DJT wasn't prepared to commit his support to an unknown candidate and was straightforward in his answer: he had the will to win and wanted to win, and he would succeed as a Republican candidate.

"It took unbelievable courage to not only make that decision, but to stand up and say it in front of millions of people across the world. But then again this is the guy who bought an amazing building at 40 Wall Street when he was in debt, interest rates were at 20 percent, and people were desperate to sell and get out. That is the measure of the guy: he does things his way."

He even brought in other members of the family to help drive the campaign beyond the boys and Ivanka doing their bit across the country. They had a campaign director in North Carolina who wasn't achieving what they wanted in the run-up to the general election. So Trump looked closer to home for a replacement. The family was on Trump's private jet, and he walked by Eric's wife, Lara, and said, "You're from North Carolina. You're in charge—congratulations!"

The job was hers.

Coming in as a producer at CBS's *Inside Edition*, it's fair to say that Lara wasn't immersed in politics the way you might imagine was necessary for a job of that nature, but Eric watched her give it her all. They saw each other about three hours a week when they were repacking their bags at home to hit the road again. She was in talks in parks and gymnasiums, and she was doing twenty towns a day.

The Trump campaign ended up winning North Carolina by 173,315 votes, an almost 4 percent margin of victory: 49.8 percent versus 46.2 percent.

"She crushed it, and we knew nothing about politics. Lara worked harder than anyone else, because she knew she had to win him that particular state."

That bravery continues to dominate the major decision making now that DJT isn't merely the boss anymore but holds the most powerful position on the planet. "To take on China and Japan head-on because we have billion-dollar trade deficits, to take on the Paris accord on climate change, because it costs us a fortune and NATO because no one else is contributing, well . . ."

Eric says social media is how Trump Senior keeps himself real and relates directly to the mom and pop in the Rust Belt, the blue-collar worker in Texas, and the retired cop in Florida. Using it, he speaks directly and clearly, without any hint of the political verbosity or flowery language that leaves people baffled. He's been knocked by everyone, according to Eric. They say his Twitter use and language isn't presidential, like when he told Kim Jong-un: "I've got nuclear weapons" and when he said, "I have a button on my desk and mine is bigger."

But for Eric, it's very simple. "What better way to deal with a bully than to punch him in the teeth, metaphorically speaking? Who would have waged a war of words with him and other leaders? He's got an innate ability to use his strength."

For Eric, the US military is the greatest in the world, and in the past, under previous leaders, it has been kept locked up and out of sight. The United States wouldn't stand up for what was right, but Eric thinks that's quickly changing. "He never cowers. He has always been good at playing the cards he has been dealt and playing them from a position of strength."

So why does Eric believe that his street brawler of a father succeeded where his slicker, practiced, and politically educated foes failed? It's clear to him. The people in that room, vying for the Republican nomination, went to the best schools, but they didn't get the sentiment of the country. They all worked for the same people and moved in the same circles, but they didn't understand what annoys and frustrates ordinary Americans—they were aloof and out of touch.

Trump is a blue-collar guy with a billion-dollar bank account. He gets people and relates to them well. He's spent his life mixing with the guys on site, the people in his restaurants and golf clubs, ordinary people who have everyday issues. It's that simple, according to Eric: he gets them.

And Eric is convinced that understanding is what got him to the top of the polls—that and the fact that fifty thousand factories left this country after Bill Clinton signed the North American Free Trade Agreement (NAFTA). People had been left behind, in Trump's view, and our education system was falling behind those in the rest of the world. He knew things need to change and understood how to get things done.

"He cuts through the crap. Look at that classic DJT maneuver with the negotiation of the proposed new Air Force Ones and the planned replacement for the F-35 in the deal with Lockheed." Sure enough, there were lots of threats, and eventually, billions of dollars got cut from these two programs alone. "He's the first guy who brought practical thinking into the administration," Eric said.

So, if the world's media is against Trump and the Left is against him, and he seems to rile the intelligentsia and the chattering classes, how can he ever truly succeed?

"He really is America's best cheerleader."

No matter if it's about golf, about business, or about building a safe world, he wants the best. He fights for what's best for the United States of America. For Eric, people know that

Trump gets results and gives what he promised and set out to do. You can't say you're a duck and be a bunny and fool someone.

The United States needed someone to go after companies to bring jobs back to the country and make American firms spend their cash at home and not store it away in offshore tax havens. Trump's confidence bred confidence, and his demands to companies not prepared to bring their wealth back to the States had evident and quick results.

For Eric, that's probably the greatest gift Trump has brought to this great nation of ours. "Some companies are very nervous of packing up and moving off. They know the risks that if you're a member of a board thinking of leaving the country to save a few dollars you could end up losing a hell of a lot more. It's Pavlov: you need to praise good behavior and condemn bad behavior; it works. It's a tool he's always used."

It's a tool Eric, Don, and Ivanka know only too well. How long can this last? Is it taking its toll on the man? There are reports of him being exhausted, realizing it's too much for him. Eric scoffed at the very thought. To him, his dad is just on the very first leg of an incredibly long journey to make America great again. And there will be a second term. "He's gonna run again," Eric said, "and by the way, he will win. He won't give up on what he's started. This is just the beginning of something truly special."

When the time comes and President Trump hands over the keys to the office to someone else to make America great again, what do Eric and his siblings think he will want to be remembered for? Will it be his achievements as president, the family he has around him, or for taking the Trump name and creating one of the biggest brands on the planet? Family is incredibly important to DJT. "He's a family guy in an unconventional way, and that's a position very few people can understand. There's never been a time in our lives that the four of us have ever broken apart. There's never been a fracture in the nucleus of Don, Ivanka, myself, and DJT, and then of course there's Tiffany and Barron, too, who will likely one day come into the family business." He knows his father would be proud of that.

"He'd better be proud of winning the presidency against all the odds and the belief of the whole world especially when we had little advantage against the others," Eric remarked.

However, Eric stopped and took stock, and as more of his executives queued up outside his glass box of an office, desperate for some of his precious time, he thought there was one accolade that Trump will always want to be remembered for more than any other. "He would want to be known as a great builder, a person who changed skylines and amassed some amazing iconic projects around the world, before anything else. He'd be proud of being president, of course, and fighting for what's right for the country, at great personal cost. But, to this day he is proudest of the things he has built and is always keen to build more. He can't help himself. That's his true and ultimate passion."

CHAPTER 24

The Twitter Traditionalist

E veryone knows that President Trump has a phone and uses Twitter, but in some respects, he's a real traditionalist who believes in the art of personal communication. He doesn't send emails and isn't a big user of computers.

It's misleading to say in this day and age that he doesn't use technology, because it's an integral part of a business for most of us. But Trump didn't have a computer on his desk, and he was more inclined to have printouts of emails handed to him to deal with. He would prefer to meet us face-to-face, look people in the eye, hear the tone of their voice, and see their body language.

In truth, there's a real art to reading people that nowadays is rapidly getting lost because it's being done through the ether. However, that ability to see people and notice their posture and body language, how they conduct themselves in a meeting, how they react under pressure, how they breathe and speak and even how they shake hands, is his preferred method of operating.

DJT worked long hours, and because of that, he was always able to give time to people—good or bad! In this day and age of computers, text, and telecoms, a lot of that personal contact—which can ultimately cement a relationship—is being lost, because there's a reluctance to engage in that way. That's not the case in the Trump Org. We know our lawyers, bankers, architects, and construction teams; we know our people, and they know us, and we ultimately get a better product in the end because of that. We were a lean, hard-hitting organization with a broad reach across many lines of business. There was no one we did not know or could not touch, and a big part of that was Trump's ability to forge incredibly tight relationships.

History will reflect on whether his Twitter use helped, hurt, or harmed him, but undoubtedly it is an efficient means to communicate directly and unfiltered with people. As Trump said once to me, "It's like owning a newspaper without the losses." I know that statement irritated some prominent editors, but I think what he meant was that by using Twitter, he was able to put his thoughts directly to the people without any editing or filtering.

When Damian and I were interviewing Trump over dinner in the White House, he reflected on his use of Twitter and knew that sometimes he was perceived as overstepping the mark. But, you know what? He is now able to engage with millions of people at once, clearly, openly, and without any misinterpretation—or downright deliberate twisting—of what he has to say. All the media laps it up, even though he's working around them.

I can say through personal experience that what can end up in print is frequently a distortion of the facts and on many occasions an outright lie. How do I know? Because I've participated in events, and what actually happened and what I then read about them have frequently been entirely different accounts—and that is in some of the most prominent and respected newspapers! For the record, I have great respect for the media and have many personal relationships built on trust and respect with individual journalists, but I have been misquoted and my actions misreported many times, and I have seen that amplified in the case of Mr. Trump. I once spent several days with a well-known, award-winning journalist who was doing a lengthy piece on one of our projects for a highly respected US magazine, only to find him misquoting all my statements, which made me out to be a liar.

And this happened to me several times.

Part of Trump's charm in person is his remarkable ability to recall people's names. It's a skill every modern president has mastered. I've seen people coming out of the office who met Trump once two years earlier, and he remembered their names: a warm, personal touch. In a society that is increasingly moving away from formal and proper social interaction, remembering and using someone's name whom you met many years ago is a touching and endearing quality and shows a certain level of respect and caring. And people like that. It's that kind of old-world charm about the guy; he comes out of his office and greets you in a waiting room with that element of respect. Today, people have lost that. They don't even get up from behind their desks when they greet you now. So despite his sometimes brash manner—and what some people would say is his rough-around-the-edges quality—here is an old-school guy who has a bundle of charm and gentlemanly qualities that many would do better to replicate or, at least, to recognize.

I can remember the first time that he met Dr. Martin Hawtree, because I had much anxiety about how the two of them would communicate and get along. Martin is a world-renowned golf course architect whose family over three generations and one hundred years has constructed or renovated more than 750 golf courses around the world, including some of the most renowned British Open venues. In the world of links course architecture, he is a rock star who remains unparalleled. However, despite these accolades, he's an extremely quiet, almost shy person. If there's a polar opposite of Donald Trump, its Martin Hawtree. So how would they get along?

We'd brought Martin in at the recommendation of the Royal and Ancient, but I was concerned about how the two men would interact. However, when they first met, they started to discuss their thoughts and ideas about how the first hole should be laid out, and it was instant mutual admiration and respect. For several hours the two of them went off on their own, and at one point, curious to know what was going on, I quietly pulled DJT aside and asked him how things were going with Martin. He said, "This guy is a genius; he's unbelievable. He may be the most talented architect I've ever worked with." Later on that day, I asked Martin the same question, and he was extremely impressed with DJT's knowledge of the game and understanding of how golf holes should be laid out.

So there you have it, two guys who are polar opposites, and they ended up collaborating on several other projects, including the renovation of Trump International Golf Club and Hotel in Doonbeg, Ireland.

DJT has a great sense of humor and is a genuinely fun person who likes to take his people out to eat, play games of golf, and reward them for the hard work they do. Damian and I managed to catch up with him at his incredible hotel in Turnberry in South Ayrshire, Scotland, during his brief visit to the United Kingdom in July 2018.

Man, was that trip fierce and controversial.

There were five hundred British cops on patrol at the hotel alone to keep the idiots at bay—although they failed when a Greenpeace activist used a parachute with a power pack strapped to his back to evade the security and fly close to the president. The Secret Service teams on tour with Trump weren't impressed by the lack of reaction from their British colleagues at all, especially when the "pilot" managed to float off into the night sky.

As DJT wandered over for a chat at the end of an evening,

dining with the likes of Woody Johnson, the US ambassa-
dor to the United Kingdom and the owner of the New York
Jets, he was full of confidence. He'd been taking on the might
of NATO over the imbalance in costs that the US felt, and
making his views known over the UK leaving the European
Union (so-called Brexit). Then he met with Her Majesty the
Queen at her private residence, Windsor Castle, just outside
London.

He was beaming from ear to ear and still full of energy,
despite the fact that the clock was showing almost eleven p.m.
Melania—as graceful and elegant as ever—wandered off to
bed, as he chatted about this book, his golf, and, of course,
the current European tour he was on. A gaggle of guests meandered over to join us and see what this man, derided by the
media and thousands of protestors in the United Kingdom,
was really like. He stopped for photos and chatted to the
guests while also keeping the conversation going with us.

Then he turned to the people swarming around him, the
Secret Service agents close by just in case, and said with a
laugh, "I've just been for tea with the queen today, what the
heck am I doing hanging around with you guys?"

It was a bit of fun that his audience really enjoyed, and
then he turned and said, "Guys, I'm off to bed, have a great
night and I'll see you tomorrow." That's the way he does
it—no airs or graces, just down-to-earth chat like he's one
of the gang and leaves folks feeling they're part of his normal life. He's very good at making people feel relaxed and
welcomed.

The next day, he did the same, stopping for photos with

supporters from North Carolina who were wearing TRUMP and MAKE AMERICA GREAT AGAIN hats, even stopping for a hug from a lady from Washington, DC, who said she was a big fan, despite where she came from. He very rarely disappoints those who want a quick word, a handshake, or a photo. He's the consummate professional.

CHAPTER 25

Cohen and the
Betrayal of DJT

Michael Cohen wasn't just a friend. He was a close friend—or at least I thought he was.

We first met in 2004 when we were involved in a board dispute at Trump World Tower. It was the sort of tough scenario that was bound to push together two like-minded people who wanted to get things done. I liked him immediately: he was aggressive, practical, and down-to-earth, and we spoke the same language.

The legal profession is a tough environment to work in; finding people you can genuinely relate to is pretty difficult, but in Michael, I thought I'd found a good guy who had the same view of the world as I did. We could work together, get things done, and have a laugh and joke along the way.

Michael and I became friends when we worked on TWT board issues together, before either of us joined The Trump Organization. Our families socialized together. I knew his kids and his brother, and when he came to the organization, I was delighted. His journey into the Trump offices almost mirrored mine: he was a lawyer whose paths had crossed with DJT's a little over the years, and he soon caught the attention of the boss.

Property was again the common factor. However, his transactions were significantly more than my one—albeit beautiful—apartment at Trump World Tower. Michael had invested in property for years, and he was a frequent buyer of Trump condominiums and high-end apartments to add to his portfolio. That kind of investment and interest doesn't go unnoticed in a sharp and agile operation like ours, and he was soon on the radar of Mr. Trump. About nine months after I left my legal practice to join The Trump Organization, Michael came through the door as a permanent member of staff, too.

Everyone knew Michael—some liked him and others didn't—but he wasn't in charge of any significant operations. He was an interesting character, and DJT seemed to be amused by his personality and work style. The suggestion that Michael was in charge of a legal department would make any other lawyer in the organization laugh out loud. However, he did have a role that could be valuable at times. For an organization to be successful, you need to have many different types of people, and sometimes there's a time for the technical, sophisticated approach, and sometimes you need a blunt object to push something through. Sure, he could be funny, a showman, and, of course, that blunt force—and that caught Mr. Trump's eye. Michael made a role for himself untangling difficult negotiations, smashing through blockages, and causing a stink to break the deadlock, but he was never a serious player in the office. He wasn't what you would describe even slightly as a fine negotiator, nor a good lawyer. Just ask those who worked alongside him. In fact, I remember Mr. Trump once telling him: "Michael, you're no diplomat."

Much of his legal work—the little he did do—was of poor quality and often had to be redrafted. And Michael would probably admit that himself. He didn't even run his own department and never managed a single project in the decade he worked for The Trump Organization. To be honest, he seemed to spend most of his time working on his outside interests.

To suggest he was some kind of mystical Svengali, or fixer, is so far wide of the mark its laughable. But he was loyal, and if there's one area that is President Trump's Achilles' heel, it's his loyalty to the people he employs.

Despite his TV persona, DJT didn't fire people at will—quite the contrary. People stay with the organization for decades; they become part of our family.

For Michael to stand up in front of Congress and claim authority over major decision making in the business was utterly ridiculous. He was hired muscle, a bluff-speaking New Yorker who could shock people into action, nothing more, nothing less. He certainly wasn't the negotiator, deal-maker, or right-hand man he portrayed himself as. That existed solely in his own mind and was the role he was so desperate to achieve—to Michael, if Trump succeeded then so did he.

Sure, he chased licensing deals and some outlandish opportunities, but that's a long way removed from getting them close to fruition. Most of them were nothing short of fantasy than anything tangible. To be honest, very few people took any notice of the suggested deals he was working on because they were so far-fetched and outlandish that we all knew they were never likely to come to fruition in a million years.

They were destined to end in failure and disappointment like so many other projects that Michael worked on.

In fact, the bitter reality for Michael is this: I know of no occasion that Michael actually secured a real estate deal, closed on a licensing opportunity, or brought any other development to a conclusion.

Not one single deal.

He just wasn't involved with the core of our business. He was a lone wolf constantly seeking the boss's approval and the proverbial pat on the back and forever fearing others would take his credit.

To be perfectly honest, his judgment just wasn't good enough to be let loose on a project in that way. There were always more trusted executives looking over his shoulder to keep him right. And everyone hated mopping up after him.

He was fun to be around, and yes, if you were a friend who needed help in the middle of the night, Michael would drop everything and step in to offer support. But that doesn't mean he was a top dog within the company; he was just a cog in the wheel—and not a very big one at that. In fact, Don,

Ivanka, and Eric avoided him as much as they could, because they were so embarrassed at his attempts to cozy up to them and seek approval.

Everyone knew that he wanted a post in the White House; it was a running joke in the company. He would mention it to so many people just about every day during the campaign and transition period, but when the boss handed over the keys and headed to 1600 Pennsylvania Avenue, Michael's raison d'être had gone.

He was never going to be chief of staff, a trusted adviser, or even one of the press team.

The fact that he was left with nothing speaks volumes.

He was obsessed with DJT and needed his attention; when that was taken from him, he was crushed.

It was clear that he no longer had a role; it was time for him to move on to pastures new, too. But, instead of walking away, Michael turned and bit the hands that fed him, postulating fictitious and exaggerated accusations that have hurt ordinary, good, honest people just trying to make a living in the company. He's thrown them to a pack of bloodthirsty wolves.

I don't say any of this to hurt Michael—he's done that to himself—I'm here to fight the corner of all those innocent people who work for The Trump Org, ordinary people like you and me, and the business itself; and yes, to fight for the president.

President Trump has succeeded in real estate development and television, and got elected to the most prestigious political post on the planet. He built an empire of dozens of residential properties and commercial projects that people love and has amassed awards and high ratings galore, along-side eleven hotels and nineteen golf courses with thousands of members. Who else can boast that? Whatever you want to say about him, very few people have achieved at the highest level in so many different industries. He's no cheat, con man, or racist; quite the opposite. And Michael knows that.

Trump had treated Michael very well for many years, pro-viding him with interesting work and life experiences. I can't accept or justify what Michael ended up doing. I no longer have any anger or negative feelings about Michael, but I can't understand why anyone—other than those with an apparent hatred against Trump and his presidency—thinks his actions should be admired. They absolutely shouldn't. To me, they represent the ultimate betrayal.

As I watched Michael give evidence to Congress, I'm sure I saw a look of regret on his face. There's no doubt in my mind that he will regret this for the rest of his life. He's going to be remembered forever for turning on his friends and those who were most loyal to him.

The whole legal system is now shocked by the actions of this man who ignored his pledges to uphold the law and act with integrity when he became a lawyer. He broke just about every fundamental principle of being a lawyer. He's certainly not a patriot.

Remember, Michael, you've been sent to prison because you lied to Congress, didn't pay your taxes, and defrauded financial institutions in your personal life—there's no one to blame for that but yourself, my friend.

CHAPTER 26

Salad, Dogs, and the Death Penalty

M any successful entrepreneurs and politicians have only one view of the people who work for them: as a means to an end, handholds to help get the boss to the top and, once there, to be forgotten. People come and people go, and many get cast off along the way.

However, DJT isn't like that. He remains loyal to his people and to his friends, no matter how high the position or the office he occupies. I never imagined I'd be in his orbit once he made it to 1600 Pennsylvania Avenue, but not only have I stopped and chatted with him on a number of occasions, but

I have also been in the White House a number of times, once dining there for this book alongside Damian.

The first time our paths crossed when he was president was about nine months after the inauguration. My role with The Trump Organization had changed somewhat. I took over handling compliance matters, battling each day to implement policies and procedures that ensured there were clean lines of separation between the organization and the executive office of the president. This work was unique and unprecedented in scale, and although the daily struggles with various members of Congress made me want to tear my hair out at times, there was a real sense of history in the making there, that I was doing something never done before.

I'd spent time with Trump that amazing day in Washington, DC, when he was sworn in, alongside my wife and friends from the operation—including Sarah Malone, who had flown over from Scotland for the event—and others from the business sector. Did I expect to be spending much time in his company after that? Not at all; he was going to be a very busy man. However, the day before Thanksgiving 2017, I was at my office in Trump International Golf Club, West Palm Beach, and he was on site, too, at what has to be one of the most beautiful and idyllic spots anywhere in the world.

My office in Palm Beach is tucked out of the way but is the perfect place for me to find peace and crack on with my daily tasks. No one bothers me there—well, apart from the world's media and every asshole from Capitol Hill who wants to bring the president and The Trump Organization down!

Although I knew Trump was going to be there, too, I didn't want to bother him. However, as is often the way with these things, I'd taken a wander over to the clubhouse to catch up with the guys and to watch the spectacle that follows Trump wherever he goes. The security is so incredible, and the size of the weapons and the sophistication of the technology is just immense. Before I even got close to the clubhouse, I was stopped by Secret Service guys and "wanded" (scanned with a handheld device to make sure I wasn't carrying anything dangerous in the vicinity of the president). There were doctors, media guys, snipers, a special Kevlar bulletproof vehicle to get him out in case of attack, and numerous dogs, cops, and agents swarming all over to ensure he remained safe.

As I was wandering along the corridors with Andy Kjos, I bumped into DJT—the most powerful man on the planet—just as he was preparing to head out to play a quick round of golf. Incidentally, boy, does he play quickly. I've never seen a guy fly around a course as quickly as he does. No messing about practicing shots; he lines them up and off he goes. Also, he's a pretty mean player—he's right up there.

His voice boomed out: "Hey, there's my guys!"

He asked Andy how he was doing and then turned to me and said, "If you're not doing anything, why don't you ride along while I play?" He was clearly trying to relax and unwind, but I'd not seen him for such a long time, and so I thought, *Why not? It'll be great to catch up with him and see what's happening.* Can you imagine that? Getting to ride alongside the president of the United States of America for an hour or two and shoot the breeze with him about what's happening in his life—that is, what's happening to keep America safe and boost one of the biggest economies on the planet!

It was a beautiful Florida day without a cloud in the sky,

one of those steaming-hot, sunny, and lovely days when you feel as if you're in paradise—except you're surrounded by guys in suits wearing sunglasses and sporting earpieces and clearly packing some heat.

One of the things that I've found the most difficult to adjust to is calling him "Mr. President." This is a man I've known for fifteen years, and he's always "Mr. Trump" to me, or "DJT," so saying "Mr. President" doesn't come easily off the tongue. However, he's not a man who makes a big deal of it; he's just happy to see friends and colleagues, people he can trust, chat to, and bounce ideas off. He does ask your opinion an awful lot about anything and everything; he wants to know what people are thinking about, what makes them tick, and how they feel about the issues of the day. It's utterly fascinating.

However, the first time I was there, it was all a bit odd. Here I was, stuck right in the middle of the presidential bubble—I was wrapped up in this craziness, the Secret Service personnel, the police, the medics, the nuclear football. Despite all these trappings, he was still the guy I knew, and he made me feel pretty comfortable, and I spent the next couple of hours on a golf cart laughing, joking, and chatting about anything and everything.

When he turned to go to the back nine, he stopped at the clubhouse to get something to drink, as any other golfer would do at every golf club in the world. However, this wasn't any other golfer, and this certainly wasn't your regular golf club you pay a few bucks to get into on a Saturday morning. As we walked into the grill room, there was a round of applause and an almighty cheer. People who knew success, some of them sports stars, many of them multimillionaires, and staff and friends alike wanted to give him the congratulations he so deserved—it wasn't contrived or false, it was just a spontaneous sense of pride and achievement among his friends, colleagues, and people he'd known for a long time. It was a moment I don't think I'll ever forget.

We also bumped into Eric, who was having a drink, and Trump asked me how Eric was doing with his company, and we joked about Eric ruining the organization that Trump had spent decades building up! He had his usual Diet Coke and then prepared to hit the course for the second half of his game. I made my apologies and said bye to both of them, as I wanted to prepare for my Thanksgiving.

As I was leaving, I mentioned I'd be in Washington the following week, and he said that if I had a minute to give him a call and stop by and say hello.

Just like that. *Stop by and say hello.*

So I did.

A few days later, I called up the White House and mentioned that I was in town and if he had a moment it would be great to see him. A few hours later I got a call and was told that I'd be able to see him at ten thirty on Wednesday morning. After going through the most incredible security, I was met by an aide who brought me into the most famous government building in the world.

Now, I'd taken a couple of public tours of the White House as a child. And as an adult, a member of the House I'd done some legal work with arranged a private tour of the White House and Capitol Hill, which was incredible. However, I never, ever contemplated that I would one day show up at the

White House and be sitting in the Oval Office with the president, which is precisely what I did that day. When I walked into the Oval Office, he said hello and told me to come in and said, "Take a look around, isn't this place great?" He spent the next few minutes explaining to me the significance of the rug, the furniture, and the paintings on the walls, the sheer history of the place—it was overwhelming.

As I sat in front of the Resolute Desk, he told me the story behind that most famous piece of furniture. It, of course, was carved out of the timbers of the abandoned and lost HMS *Resolute*, a British warship that was rediscovered by a US vessel and returned to Queen Victoria as a gesture of friendship and goodwill. She had the timbers made into a desk at Chatham Dockyard in my country of birth and presented to President Rutherford Hayes in 1880.

He asked me what I thought, and I told him that as someone who'd been born in another country and arrived in the United States by boat when he was a small child, I could never have imagined that I would be sitting in this place with my friend, the president. It was just another example of how great this country is, where even people who immigrate there can find themselves sitting somewhere like that. It's something we Americans take for granted.

We talked for a few moments about recent politics and sports, and, unsurprisingly, he asked me what I thought about certain world events, but then he was getting ready to leave for a speaking engagement outside Washington, and so I wished him well and said I'd probably see him around Christmastime. I think every person I knew on earth that day heard the story that I was in the Oval Office, I was that excited. I hadn't walked back to my hotel before I'd called twenty different people.

There were a string of other meetings, some formal and some just by chance, at which I managed to catch a few words with President Trump, too.

Around Christmastime there was a family fun day at West Palm Beach. I brought my son to meet the forty-fifth president of the United States of America, and they fist-bumped on the golf course! There were so many people in the place, but I grabbed a cart and took my son and intercepted the president as he was playing. My son fist-bumped him, and we spent five minutes talking. My son, only four years old at the time, still speaks of that day and says President Trump is "his president." That will remain with him forever.

I've seen Trump a few times when he's been at the club, sometimes merely to chat with him for a few minutes, but in February 2018, Damian and I went to have a proper lunch with him in Florida for this book. We'd spent the week immediately prior gathering our thoughts, communicating with Hope Hicks, the former director of communications for the White House, and other members of the White House to ensure we had the necessary clearance and could pass through the phalanx of security to get close to the man himself. In The Trump Organization, access was encouraged and straightforward. We usually just walked down the hallway to his office. Now it's more complicated, but the bottom line is, in reality, it hasn't changed at all. You may have to jump through a hoop or two, but if I reach out to speak to him, it's reciprocated; he's still open and still wants his friends to talk to him. There's still a feeling of excitement whenever I get to chat with him again, despite the fact I've known him for so long.

When you head to West Palm Beach, you see Air Force One parked at Palm Beach International; there's no outward sign of anything unusual. As you approach the golf course—where for the past couple of years my base has been and where my office is—everything seems normal and quiet. There's nothing that would suggest that the president is inside, but as soon as you come to the front gates, you can tell that things are different.

The weather as ever was warm and sunny, but being February, it wasn't too hot. Even my Limey friend could cope with that! We arrived at the main entrance, and the security guard on duty knew we were expected, as he said, "You guys having lunch with the president, eh?" And he waved us on through. The blacktop was full to overflowing with Secret Service agents, sheriff's vehicles, and local police officers, not to mention some of the most sinister-looking trucks and SUVs I've ever seen. There were cops everywhere and the usual cacophony of agents chatting to each other and whispering into the microphones placed neatly in their sleeves.

What was odd was that this scene didn't seem to distract the members and their families, who carried on as usual—their day was about making the most of it while they had some spare time on a Saturday morning to play their beloved sport. Andy Kjos, the course superintendent, felt it, though, because afterward he has to repair all the fairways and boundaries to the cart path from the hefty Secret Service vehicles bouncing along at high speed as they protect the president.

The Secret Service guys form the highly specialized teams

that are prepared for every scenario: medical teams, snipers, bomb-sniffing dogs, and the like. On the back of a golf cart, there was a dog cage that toured the course in advance of his party to physically check each hole, tee box, fairway, and green for any sign of explosive devices. Then, watching from a discreet distance, with the biggest pair of military binoculars you'll ever see, and with some of the most potent and massive rifles, the antisniper team was always on the lookout and prepared to deal with an attack.

Alongside them were other tactical teams that can handle chemical attacks, antiassault teams, and the military attaché with the nuclear football no more than a few yards away. Also trailing behind was a peculiar John Deere farm vehicle with a trailer attached to the rear that's made of Kevlar, which, according to one of the agents, would have been used in the event of a complete assault. They would have put the president into this weird little green trailer on the back of a tractor and covered him with a bulletproof blanket and driven him the hell out of there. It's not particularly graceful or presidential, but if the shit hits the fan, it's a great way to get someone out under covering fire.

It's probably worth noting that there was so much more security that we weren't even aware of.

The White House photographer was in the convoy, too, but it's all very organized and not intimidating and not disruptive for other members, as these guys are so good at what they do. It's an amazingly calm environment when you're in that inner bubble; it's actually a tranquil place. To get into the middle of it all, you need to be vetted in advance, and on the day of the meeting you pass through multiple layers of security. Being in there with the president is probably the safest place on the planet to be. You get wanded wherever you go, and there's a lot of eyes on you. I once asked a Secret Service agent jokingly what he would do if I were to lunge at the president. He responded, "I would shoot you, sir." Point taken.

After going through the security, we waited a while and chatted to various members of the advance team. It's incredible how polite, professional, and young most of these men and women are—they are so enthusiastic about what they're doing. They're so into it, and to me, it's evident that they realize the importance of what they're doing. They're very proud of it, and that comes out in the way they behave and treat others. These are the best of the best. The country owes them a tremendous debt of gratitude and much respect.

We watched Trump play at different spots on the golf course—with about thirty-plus golf carts in attendance—and waited for him to come off the course. He gave us his usual happy welcome, asking how his guys were and what was happening in our worlds. We wandered with him into the clubhouse, no different than we would on any other day, but on this particular day, the focus of the discussion was this book.

At one o'clock, we walked into the grill room, and it being a Saturday afternoon, it was full of members and their guests. On the way to the table we bumped into Jimmy Connors— yes, that Jimmy Connors. Here it was again, no private room, just sitting at the table with everyone else. Trump chatted to quite a few people on the way in. The machine, the Washington insiders, the swamp creatures, are uncomfortable with the fact that the president is out there mixing with ordinary people, the members, staff, and golf crew. He knows every one of these guys by name and takes the time to give them a couple of words, and they love him for it.

He asked the waitress Rosie whether a favorite soup was on the menu and she said it wasn't on until tomorrow, it was a lunch buffet, and he could help himself. Just like that. No "Yes, Mr. President, I'll get whatever you want," or "Right away, Mr. President." Nope, Rosie has known him for years, and she told him like he was just any other member of the club. "It's a buffet, and you can go and help yourself."

He was more than happy with that. He hopped up and went over to help himself. He got a crab salad and pickles—we had hot dogs, fries, and pickles. That's right; he was enjoying a big, fresh salad. Don't believe everything you read in the papers.

(For the record, the grilled hot dogs at any Trump property—and I consider myself a hot dog connoisseur—are the best, hands down.)

The conversation jumped around from the possibility of the death penalty for drug dealers to Brexit, a lot on Twitter, what we were doing, how our lives were, and asking about the economy and my views on politics in the United Kingdom. Trump was genuinely interested in a lot of ordinary things.

On the issue of drug dealing, he was consumed with the fact that tens of thousands of Americans were dying every year because of drugs. He seemed determined to be the guy who finally did something about it. So many people have talked about it, from Reagan's famous declaration of war to the continuous pumping of money into tackling the sources of drugs in the United States. As the father of two children, I can say that drugs are something I worry about all the time—

I'm not talking about a joint here and there, I'm talking about heroin and the prescription opioid pills that are ravaging our country.

Spend time with the man and you can see how much he cares about this. It's not an act. It invades his time off. He's merely sitting quietly with friends and talking; he's asking people what they think. The things we talked about haven't changed, and it's a source of frustration—he's still out there talking to the guys on the street, as he always has done.

As we were sitting there, people invariably stopped by to say hello and apologize about taking photos with him, but he was cool about it. A friend of mine, Stephen Jara, was running for a local position in Palm Beach County, and his name appeared on a ballot alongside Trump's. I explained the situation to the president, and he was delighted to write him a nice note and sign the ballot, because that's just the kind of guy he is.

As quickly as it began, after forty-five minutes or so, it was time for him to head off back to Mar-a-Lago and carry on with the business of state. He knew we wanted a bit more time with him later on, and he said to get in touch and arrange it. It was that simple. He gave us a pat on the back, shook our hands, took a couple of photos, and then was away in his massive convoy of bullet- and bombproof SUVs.

The president had left the building.

CHAPTER 27

Walking into the White House

A few days later, Damian and I were in Washington, DC, and we met up with Hope Hicks, then the director of communications for the White House. At about 3:40 p.m., as the cold and drizzle permeated the Washington air, we checked into the northwest entrance to go through the security screening necessary to get into the West Wing—where all the political operations occur and where the Oval Office is. As a foreign national, Damian required some time to be afforded the necessary clearance and had to be escorted onto the property by one of the young associates who had been part of the team since the inauguration.

As we entered the building, tucked into a corner out of sight of the main road, to the right of the front of the White House, we were greeted by marines dressed in full ceremonial attire with the most polished shoes imaginable.

We had to hang our coats up—it was damp and incredibly cold—and put our mobile phones into a locker before we were asked to take a seat in a beautifully attired waiting room close to the Oval Office. On the wall right beside us was a very handsome painting of John Tyler, the tenth president. Elsewhere on the walls were paintings of battles and ships from the early days of this great nation, and of the earliest Americans to inhabit the land.

The carpet was a gentle beige and patterned, and the area had a feel of relaxed comfort—almost like a small, exclusive, five-star hotel lobby—and the place was incredibly quiet. We were offered coffee, water, or soda by a receptionist but had to wait just a short few minutes before Hope emerged from her domain. A beautiful bunch of yellow roses dominated the entrance hall on the reception desk. Hope was so full of energy and was immaculately dressed. Her voice is not something many people have heard, and she's rather quiet, slightly high pitched, and very charming.

"Hi, Georgie!" She beamed and remembered Damian from a previous trip to Scotland during the presidential campaign.

We walked along a narrow corridor toward the main White House building and diverted off to the left toward her office. To the right, through a corridor often seen on TV as leading to the Oval Office, were a plethora of Secret Service guys guarding the hall.

As we turned left, there was the personal secretary to President Trump, Madeleine Westerhout, at her large desk. The place has an air of youthfulness about it: Madeleine and Hope were still in their twenties.

As we turned right toward the Oval Office, we passed Hope's tiny office, which was no more than ten by eight feet. Imagine spending long chunks of your day in an office that small with no natural light—it must have driven her crazy! There was barely room for a desk and a couple of chairs. However, that's probably the best office in the building; it's right next to the president. Location, location, location.

As we chatted about her requirements for our meeting with the president, she was batting off calls and emails on her cell phone. The place was calm and measured, but it must have been frenetic. There was no sense of the madness that the media would have you believe pervades the place. It seemed that it was just like any other busy office, except you happened to be next to the most important and recognizable working office on the planet. We discussed dates for our next meeting and chatted about people we knew and how we'd get back so that we could see DJT.

After some more pleasantries, we hopped out of the office and there on the right was the open door to the Oval Office. Hope had already asked if the boss was close by for us to pop in and say hi, but Madeleine said he was in a meeting with Republican senators (talks about another government shutdown were ongoing). He wasn't in, but we could see the famous Resolute Desk, and his chair, which he'd had shipped in from his office in Trump Tower. It was pretty amazing to be in the doorway of the Oval Office, just a few short feet away from the ultimate seat of power. It's an awful lot smaller than you imagine it to be and than it seems on TV, but it exudes power and authority. There's a real stillness and calm about the whole environment.

CHAPTER 28

Standing on the Shoulders of Giants

Dinner at the White House is a strange event. I flew in from Florida and Damian came in from the United Kingdom, and we met up at the Old Post Office, more formally known as Trump International Hotel Washington, DC, which seemed like it had become a home away from home.

We had a relaxed dinner the night before and talked about how we would approach what was becoming clear would be a unique meeting: we were having a private dinner in the White House with the president of the United States, who

also happened to be a trusted friend. There was much anticipation. For me, a guy who immigrated to the United States as
a youngster, this was something that was beyond my realm
of expectation, and although I set my goals very high, a private dinner meeting in the Blue Room with the sitting president of the United States wasn't something I would ever have
imagined. There's not a single person in my world—even my
extended business and social circle—who had ever done anything like that.

On that day, with everything swirling from trade wars, issues on the Korean Peninsula, the firing of cabinet members,
the expelling of Russian diplomats, and all manner of things
that the president faces on a daily basis, he took time to see
us, and that means a lot. It would have been straightforward
for him to avoid us and instead focus on something much
more important. He ended up giving us almost two hours
of his precious time on the day that he was involved in a
multitude of complex diplomatic matters, including a tense
telephone conversation with Theresa May—the prime minister
of the country of my birth—over her handling of Brexit.

We woke up on the morning of the dinner and took a walk
around Washington, swinging by Capitol Hill, and somehow
ended up at Ford's Theater—the site, obviously, of Lincoln's
assassination—not knowing that just a few hours later we
would be standing in Lincoln's bedroom in the White House,
openmouthed.

We stumbled on a lovely Washington restaurant while still
dressed in jeans. The place was full of middle-aged, fat politicos, dressed in their ill-fitting but ridiculously expensive
suits, looking down their noses at us, with our plastic bags

full of souvenirs for our kids. Little did they know that the only two guys in that nest of vipers who were ever going to sit down for a private and intimate dinner in the White House with the most powerful man on the planet were us.

There was even a cabinet member (who was later fired in the most dramatic and inglorious fashion) holding court in his own corner as a string of flunkeys and wannabe highfliers kissed his ring on the way in and out. It was horrible to watch and kind of sums up everything that's bad about the government machine in our wonderful country. Take note: you never know who the person sitting next to you is, and don't be so presumptuous as to judge people on how they look.

Both Damian and I felt a palpable sense of self-importance and arrogance spewing forth from these politicos as they whispered, plotted, and gossiped around us. I understand how people could really hate Washington, DC—or, more particularly, the swamp, as it's known. Everywhere you turned, there were former diplomats, analysts, and politicos saying why the president had been wrong in his handling of North Korea.

We'd been instructed by White House staff to report to the northeast gate at 6:15 p.m. When we approached the entrance in the pouring rain, we were promptly informed by the Secret Service that there was no record of us having any business there and were asked whom we had an appointment with. It felt strange to reply that we were there for dinner with the president himself, and the agent looked at us and smiled in disbelief. It's probably something he hears from hundreds of nutcases who come by and say it every day. I even felt stupid saying the words, but, bizarrely, it was the truth.

After a couple of minutes and a couple of phone calls, the issue was resolved, and we received word that we had been cleared, but not before the same Secret Service guard looked at us incredulously and said, "But there are only two guests for this dinner." We both said almost in unison, "That's right, that's us." We were quickly and smartly ushered through!

We were met by a couple of smiling young staffers at the east entrance, who were eager to give us information about the history of this fantastic place. As you walk in and head down the East Wing Corridor and onto a sumptuously carpeted hallway to the main body of the White House, you pass long, grand marble corridors filled with giant photos and beautiful oil paintings of current and past first families. There's even a massive painting of Hillary Clinton with her usual smug grin bearing down on you.

We took an elevator up a floor and emerged into the most amazing and grand reception hall, the Cross Hall, which sits immediately behind that lantern on the outside of the front of the building—probably the most famous house lantern on the planet. There are crystal chandeliers, marble columns, and a beautiful, regal red carpet. Walking through it, you are watched over by Washington, Jefferson, Lincoln, Kennedy, Bush—the whole cadre of former presidents witnessing your every move. This fantastic hall, the reception area for world dignitaries, also boasts a stunning Steinway piano, presented to the United States, and some incredible clocks and mirrors to add to the air of grandeur there.

Our reception by the members of the White House dining staff was impeccable and so friendly. It was incredible talking to these guys, some of whom had served nine presidents and been there for more than forty years. They were so enthusiastic, proud, and full of information, the most wonderfully welcoming people—I can't tell you how happy we were to speak to them, and we regretted not being able to take a group photo with them. We couldn't thank them enough for what they were doing for us.

It was fascinating to talk to them about which former presidents they liked and to get a few stories about some of the highlights in their long and distinguished services—no one could have been prouder of their place in the White House, and yet they were so humble about it.

We were allowed to wander through various state reception rooms, including the Blue Room, where we were to have our private dinner with the president—and what was really striking was that the table wasn't the kind found at your usual, massive banquet facility, but a small, beautiful oval table with just three classy but straightforward place settings for us! The only difference between our layout and his was that DJT's condiments were more prominent, of course, and placed directly in front of his place rather than to the left, like ours were.

It was just beautifully elegant.

The hushed room is round and has ornate blue drapes and, of course, a thick blue carpet with gold flowers, and it boasts more paintings of presidents from the past watching serenely over you. You could hear a pin drop, and yet we were in the middle of one of the most important and busiest cities on the planet—I guess that bulletproof glass also keeps the noise out! Whenever I go to the White House, I always feel so amazingly safe. Even though you are sitting right beside one of the most targeted men in the world, you know that you are never in any danger.

To the right of the Blue Room is the East Room, with a huge dining table and an iconic painting of George Washington, which, if you look very carefully (we were told) boasts a spelling error in it and was saved from the flames when the British tried to burn the White House. The painting was a copy and was whisked away by the artist himself, Gilbert Stuart, before the attack, who gave it a deliberate spelling error—in the words "United States"—to differentiate it from the original. Wherever you look in the White House, there are incredible monuments to history and the people who have graced those hallowed halls. Constant reminders are all around of the magnitude and gravity of events that have taken place there over the decades.

After one false alarm when we all jumped to attention as a Secret Service agent prematurely announced the president was on his way, there was a definite buzz as we heard a huddle of people heading our way up the stairs from the West Wing.

He was preceded by only a couple of agents a few steps in front of him, which struck us as slightly low key. And then there he was, striding toward us with his usual casual style and saying, "Hey, here's my guys," and uttering, "So, what do you think of this place?"

Damian asked him how he was, and with a slight sigh he said, "Well, I've had better days."

You know, there he was, clearly tired and with a lot on his mind, but he was still keen to chat with friends and put all the stresses to one side.

He ushered us into the Blue Room with a cheery "Come

on, let's go and sit down," and we took our places in our designated spots, with presidents from the beginning of the history of our great nation watching down on us and our view through the windows out toward the Washington monument.

It was all so surreal.

At the core, he was the same person we knew, and in reality, that dinner could have been at any time in the past in New York, Florida, Scotland, or Ireland. However, he did bring with him a certain somberness and gravitas, which comes with the territory. So while things seemed the same, they also were very different. At heart, he was the same man we knew, but this was also the forty-fifth president of the United States of America, and clearly, something had changed. He'd grown into the role and seemed both equally at home while also having that somber weight of expectation that the post brings with it. As we chatted, he even admitted that the role was more than he believed it would be to begin with, but that he'd grown into it over the preceding months and was now pushing on with the challenge with real relish. "We're now way ahead of schedule," he said.

This wasn't just Mr. Trump the businessman, this was a new President Trump, the leader of the free world, with the gravitas and seriousness the office demands. The difference was subtle but nonetheless utterly palpable.

The conversation ebbed and flowed about friends and foes past and present, the inevitable politics, and life as the president of the United States of America. All the while, a Secret Service agent hovered at the doorway watching discreetly, ready to pounce should anything go wrong.

We discussed some of the headlines and significant issues, and the subject of China came up. He made the point that he had great respect for Xi Jinping, president of the People's Republic of China, and a mighty man indeed.

Hey, he has the fate of one-and-a-half billion people in his hands.

DJT said that he thrived on his conversations with President Xi, that he was extremely knowledgeable, and he reflected on how complex the trade negotiations were. "Xi Jinping is a good guy; he's tough, but I can work with him."

While culturally Xi Jinping and Donald Trump are as different as you can get, at the core they are very similar: two no-nonsense leaders who view the world through a singular lens. They see only what's best for their countries, but they are smart and practical enough to recognize that one cannot thrive without being in harmony with the other. The United States needs China, and China needs the United States. Unlike our bloated cronies from the restaurant that day in Washington, who will waste months and millions of dollars talking, analyzing, perseverating, and bullshitting, the two of them will sit down and get it done. These are two dominant personalities going full speed at each other—for example, in the trade talks—but their aggression is tempered by practical intelligence and never losing sight of the end goal, which is to make a deal. They both respect each other, despite their differences, and know that a deal will be done.

From my perspective, this is what leadership is all about. It's refreshing to see this approach on a world stage, and I can understand that it's unsettling to the establishment, but as the 2016 election proved beyond any doubt, the majority of Americans agree with me. As we continued to talk about world leaders, Damian asked him about a visit from the French president, Emmanuel Macron, and Trump said, "I really like Emmanuel, he's been good to us. . . ."

While he held a certain healthy respect for the challenges and troubles other politicians found themselves in, he wasn't so enamored with them. Prime Minister Theresa May of the United Kingdom was one premier he believed had incredibly tricky negotiations to face with Brexit, but he felt she hadn't been as robust or as direct as she should have been, or as he would have been. "I would have done it a whole lot differently," he said. "And I would have got a much stronger deal than is being proposed."

As we all gently ate through our first course—beautiful sea scallops and lemon pasta—he ruminated on the whole environment he now found himself in, and in a moment of self-reflection quietly pondered the people who'd been in his chair before. He said he found the responsibility almost daunting. "I feel the weight of history on me, for sure, but I'm standing on the shoulders of giants. . . ." His tone was calm, quiet, and measured, and he expressed his admiration for the titans who had come before him. He was clear that he had sacrificed a lot to take on the role but felt that he needed to do it for the benefit of the United States and to use the skills he'd garnered as a businessman over the past five decades. "I felt I could do a good job and this country has been heading down the wrong path for a long time. Not only do our enemies take advantage of us but so do our friends. That has to stop.

"I see things differently than others, and I could see we were heading down a dangerous path and I had to stop and change that no matter what it cost me."

However, he felt that if he'd been a Biden, or a Sanders, or even a Hillary, he would have had far less criticism at the hands of the press. That wasn't him feeling sorry for himself or whining about it; it was just a reflection on how he was treated. Inevitably, the issue of Twitter cropped up. He's been told by close friends that he should tone it down a bit, but he believes Twitter lets him get straight to the people who matter—the voters—without having to be filtered by third parties who have their own anti-Trump agenda.

"Listen, today I fired a cabinet member and revealed it on Twitter to the world and the media was all over it in seconds. . . . It's a modern form of communication, and I can speak directly to the people without anyone changing the meaning or sense of my words."

Then, as we ate our main course of thyme-brined chicken breast, shallot jus, and spring vegetable fricassee, we delved into a discussion as to which was worse: the *New York Times* or the *Washington Post*. My view was that they're each as pompous as the other, but the *Washington Post* is just in a gutter all by itself. I know this isn't going to help with the book reviews in any way, but having dealt firsthand with many of its journalists, that's how I feel: the *Washington Post* is a self-righteous gutter newspaper that very few people now even care about or find interesting. It's nothing more than a left-wing hit publication that looks down on middle-class

America and caters to a narrow ruling class that couldn't care less about the average Joe Smith.

We could have been sitting, like so many times in the past, on a construction site, or in his New York office, or on his plane, but this time we were enjoying the most exquisite food in the most exclusive dining establishment on the planet. There was no steak, fries, or burgers in sight—and this was the president of the United States, not Mr. Trump. He was wearing his trademark blue suit, for sure, a red, black, and blue striped tie, and a crisp white shirt, but the little clues gave it away: the number forty-five embroidered on the cuff, with diamond cufflinks.

He was proud of what he had achieved and was clear that he was going to keep driving forward. "I do miss certain things about my former life, but I've no regrets about going for this job and winning; I don't like to regret anything."

As we finished dessert—warm honey-glazed puff pastry, pears and blueberries, and salted caramel ice cream—he asked us if we had a minute, as he wanted to show us something. We casually walked upstairs as we continued chatting, again past some amazing oil paintings, and wandered into the heart of his private residence, decorated with beautiful creams and hues of various shades of warm yellow and boasting magnificent bouquets of tulips and other flowers to add to its charm. It oozed elegance, calm, and comfort.

Then we were shown into a room that contained Lincoln's desk and a portrait of the signing of the Louisiana Purchase, and then, even more incredibly, into Lincoln's bedroom, which contained a huge bed—remember he was six feet, four inches—and the original copy of the Gettysburg Address, held behind bulletproof glass.

It was astonishing.

There it was: "Four score and seven years ago . . ."

As I mentioned earlier, President Trump reminded us that at the time the speech received mixed reviews but within fifty years was considered the greatest speech ever. How telling was that? There are many instances of people not getting the credit they deserve from their contemporaries and then only later, when the rose-tinted glasses come off, do they get that credit.

Trump gave us that brief but heartfelt history lesson about the artifacts in the room and seemed to be genuinely touched by the tragedy that enveloped Lincoln's life, especially the death of his son Willie.

The thing that stuck in my head after we shook hands and started to part ways was that again Trump said to keep in touch and to wish his best to our families. As we walked down the stairs toward the exit, he turned and walked into his private residence, and the Secret Service details gently closed the thick glass doors behind him as his back disappeared into the distance. It was a lockdown for the night, and no one was getting in.

Once again, we were guided downstairs, in elevators and along those fantastic corridors to be deposited into the street beyond. We said our goodbyes to his assistants and then passed back through security into the dark of the world outside. The building looked so beautiful lit up at night, and I so wanted to share it with my son. I called him on FaceTime and took a few photos.

Amid all the tourists milling about in the cold night air,

there was a family there, doing what we were doing, posing and taking photos, and I overheard one of them saying: "I wonder if President Trump is in there?"

I laughed to myself as I thought, *Yup, he's in there all right . . .*

And then we wandered off into the drizzle of the night.

Acknowledgments

We offer grateful thanks to the following for their time, guidance, stories, humor, and fortitude!

To the forty-fifth president of the United States of America, Donald J. Trump, for giving us his time when it is the most precious commodity he has.

To Donald Trump Jr., Eric Trump, Sarah Malone, Meredith McIver, Hope Hicks, Keith Schiller, Paul Werther, and Eric Nelson and his wonderful team at HarperCollins: Thank you all for your patience, understanding, assistance, guidance, and support.

To Alan Garten, Amanda Miller, Andy Kjos, Mike Vergara, Andy Billik, and Oren Kattan for your great stories and insights. Thank you to Cynthia Arce for coordinating everything and getting us there on time.

To Scott Goodman and David Waizer for your advice and friendship.

To Mickael Damelincourt, Daniel Mahdavian, and all the team at OPO—a home from home.

To the Coptic Orthodox Church for teaching me the power of faith and for being at my side each day.

To our wives and young children: Sorry for the long absences and long-distance phone calls. We couldn't have done it without your love and support.

And thank you to you for blocking out the white noise and realizing there's more to DJT than the media would have you believe. This book is for you.

About the Authors

GEORGE A. SORIAL was Executive Vice President & Counsel to The Trump Organization for over twelve years, working directly alongside Donald J. Trump until his inauguration in January 2017. He then became EVP and Chief Compliance Counsel to the business, reporting directly to Donald Trump Jr. and Eric Trump.

Throughout his tenure with The Trump Organization, Mr. Sorial held senior management responsibility for the acquisition, development, and construction of numerous mixed-use projects, including the highly acclaimed Trump International Golf Links, Scotland property.

He was formerly an associate with the Day Pitney law firm and a partner with DeCotiis, Fitzpatrick and Cole, LLP.

He earned a juris doctor degree from Boston University School of Law, an MBA from Boston University Graduate School of Management, and an LLM from Seton Hall Law School.

DAMIAN BATES has been a journalist in the UK for almost thirty years. He was a newspaper editor for over a decade and was also editor-in-chief of a group of newspapers and digital platforms in Scotland. He was a leading member of a number of UK-based newspaper-industry groups and regulatory bodies. He now runs his own reputation management consultancy, covering strategic communications, strategic leadership, and public affairs. He is a mentor, visiting professor, and international marketing company chairman. He has known Donald J. Trump for over a decade. For the record, he is married to Sarah Malone.